AUG 2 2 2006

W9-BLI-921

WITHDRAWN

AL-KHWARIZMI

The Inventor of Algebra

Great Muslim Philosophers and Scientists of the Middle Ages™

AL-KHWARIZMI

The Inventor of Algebra

Corona Brezina

The Rosen Publishing Group, Inc., New York

Published in 2006 by The Rosen Publishing Group, Inc.
29 East 21st Street, New York, NY 10010

First Edition

Library of Congress Cataloging-in-Publication Data
Brezina, Corona.
Al-Khwarizmi: the inventor of algebra/Corona Brezina.—1st ed.
     p. cm.—(Great Muslim philosophers and scientists of the Middle Ages)
Includes bibliographical references.
ISBN 1-4042-0513-6 (lib. bdg.)
1. Khwarizmi, Muhammad ibn Msa?, fl. 813–846. 2. Muslim scientists—
     Biography. 3. Mathematics, Arab.
I. Title. II. Series.
Q143.K4B74 2006
509'.2—dc22
                                                                2005018449

Manufactured in the United States of America

On the cover: A postage stamp featuring a portrait of al-Khwarizmi.

3 1558 00226 8175

CONTENTS

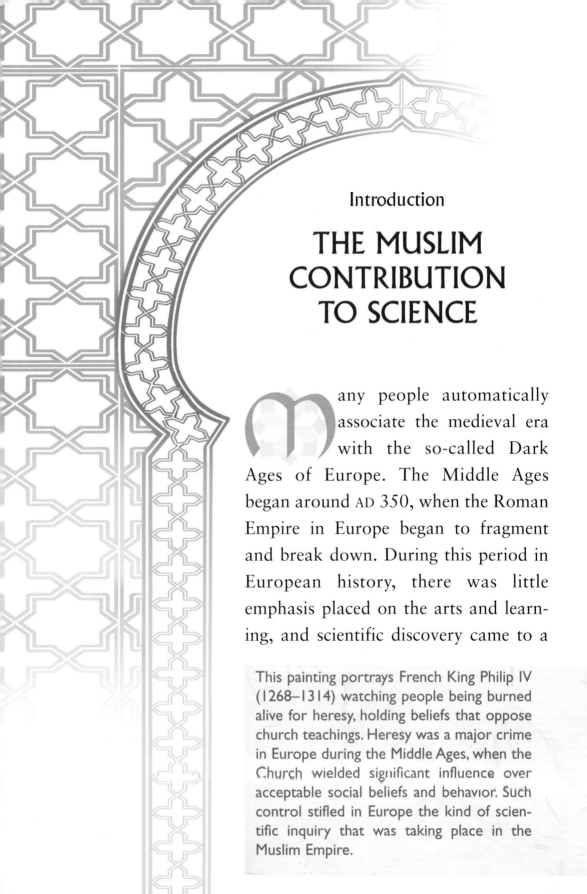

Introduction

THE MUSLIM CONTRIBUTION TO SCIENCE

Many people automatically associate the medieval era with the so-called Dark Ages of Europe. The Middle Ages began around AD 350, when the Roman Empire in Europe began to fragment and break down. During this period in European history, there was little emphasis placed on the arts and learning, and scientific discovery came to a

This painting portrays French King Philip IV (1268–1314) watching people being burned alive for heresy, holding beliefs that oppose church teachings. Heresy was a major crime in Europe during the Middle Ages, when the Church wielded significant influence over acceptable social beliefs and behavior. Such control stifled in Europe the kind of scientific inquiry that was taking place in the Muslim Empire.

ce luv ditho feu schol elne renduo
quanque il auoit saisi du leur · Cy sine
le second liure du noble Roy philipe dieudom

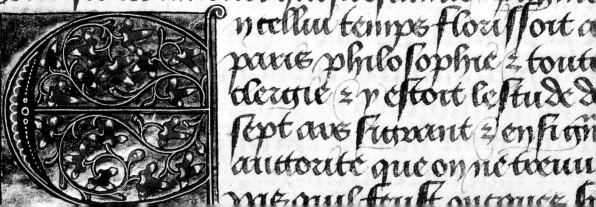

De lerefie des amoriet qui fu estamte z pugme
n icellui temps florissort a
paris philosophie z toute
clergie z y estort lestude de
sept aus suyuant z en si gn̄
auttorite que on ne teuoit
nes nul fruct autoiet

grinding halt. There would not be a major intellectual reawakening until around the twelfth century, when the Italian Renaissance ushered in a revival of classical Greek and Roman culture and spread throughout Europe. Few members of the population were educated during these Dark Ages, and little scholarly work was done outside Catholic monasteries.

Within two centuries of its emergence in Mecca in the seventh century, Islam had spread rapidly across Arabia and into Africa, Central Asia, and even Europe through a combination of conversion and military conquest. This map of the Muslim Empire shows its territorial reach at two points in history: around AD 700, nearly seven decades after Muhammad's rule; and around 850, when the empire was at its greatest extent.

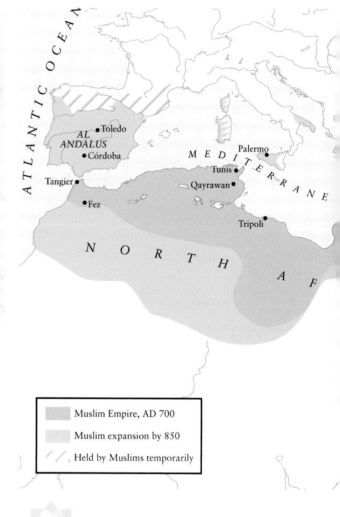

Muslim Empire, AD 700

Muslim expansion by 850

Held by Muslims temporarily

While the Roman Empire faltered and crumbled in Europe, the vast Muslim Empire began spreading throughout the Middle East and North Africa, eventually extending all the way to Spain and India. As the empire grew, its scholars began collecting knowledge from the conquered cultures. This harvesting of intellectual works led to Islam's golden age of cultural and scientific achievement, which lasted

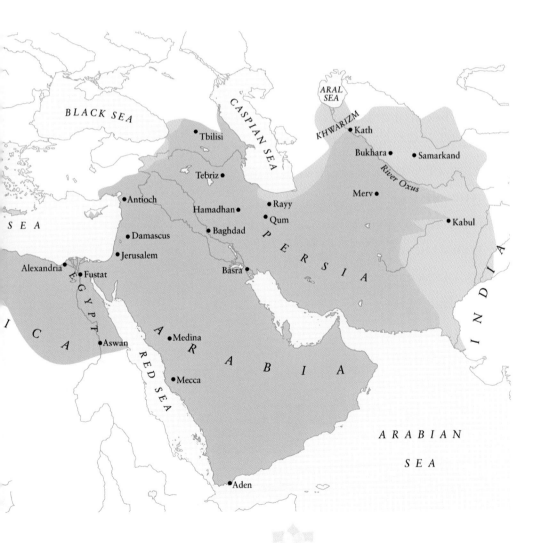

from about 750 to 1258. Within the great city of Baghdad (in present-day Iraq), Muslim rulers encouraged scholars to translate scientific and philosophical texts into Arabic. Scientists then used them to support their own research. Baghdad rapidly became one of the most sophisticated cities of the world, and Muslim scholars made important advances in mathematics, astronomy, geography, and many other sciences. When Europeans finally emerged from the Dark Ages, the translated texts and scientific progress of Islam's golden age helped fuel Europe's own Renaissance.

One of the most influential figures of Muslim science was the ninth-century astronomer, mathematician, and geographer al-Khwarizmi. Al-Khwarizmi lived in Baghdad during the reign of Caliph al-Mamun, a great supporter of science and the arts. Al-Khwarizmi worked at the House of Wisdom, an academy established by al-Mamun for research and translation of classic texts of antiquity. Scholars at the House of Wisdom studied and translated the works of Greece, Babylonia, and other cultures. Al-Khwarizmi drew on Hindu sources for two of his major works.

Al-Khwarizmi is best remembered for his famous work *Kitab al-Jabr wal-Muqabala* (The Compendius Book on Calculation by Completion and Balancing), the text that defined the branch of mathematics known as algebra. The word "algebra" is derived from the title of al-Khwarizmi's work. Mathematicians of other cultures had developed some basic algebraic concepts, but al-Khwarizmi was the first mathematician to present the elements of algebra in a systematic form.

Al-Khwarizmi's other great mathematical work was his treatise on Hindi numerals. The "Arabic" system of numbers used today is of Hindi origin. Al-Khwarizmi's treatise explained the decimal place value system and the concept of zero. Centuries after his death, it was translated into Latin and became influential in introducing Hindi numerals to Europe. The Latin translation was titled *Algoritmi de Numero Indorum*, (Al-Khwarizmi Concerning the Hindi Art of Reckoning). "Algoritmi" was a Latin transcription of "al-Khwarizmi," but the word gradually changed in spelling and meaning. The modern term "algorithm" is derived from al-Khwarizmi's name.

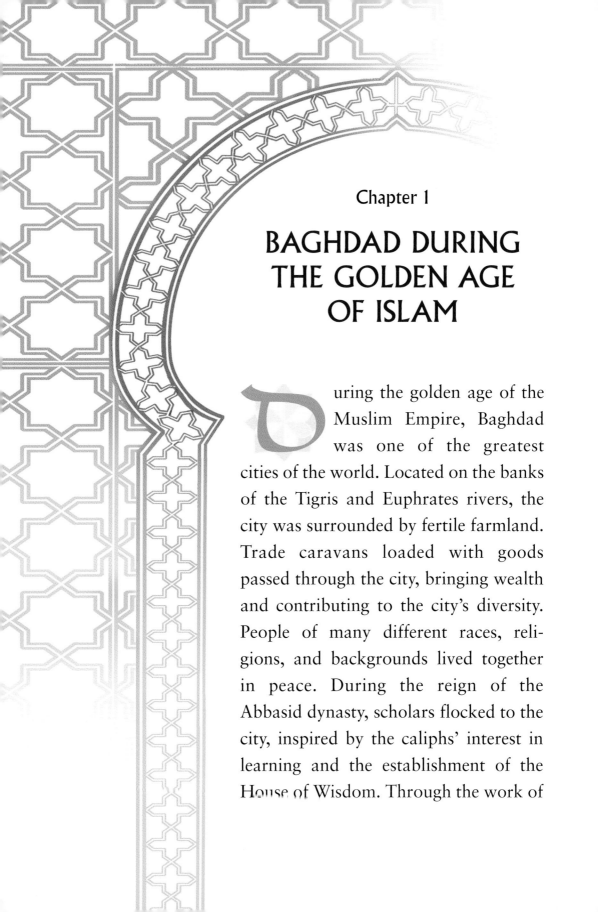

Chapter 1

BAGHDAD DURING THE GOLDEN AGE OF ISLAM

uring the golden age of the Muslim Empire, Baghdad was one of the greatest cities of the world. Located on the banks of the Tigris and Euphrates rivers, the city was surrounded by fertile farmland. Trade caravans loaded with goods passed through the city, bringing wealth and contributing to the city's diversity. People of many different races, religions, and backgrounds lived together in peace. During the reign of the Abbasid dynasty, scholars flocked to the city, inspired by the caliphs' interest in learning and the establishment of the House of Wisdom. Through the work of

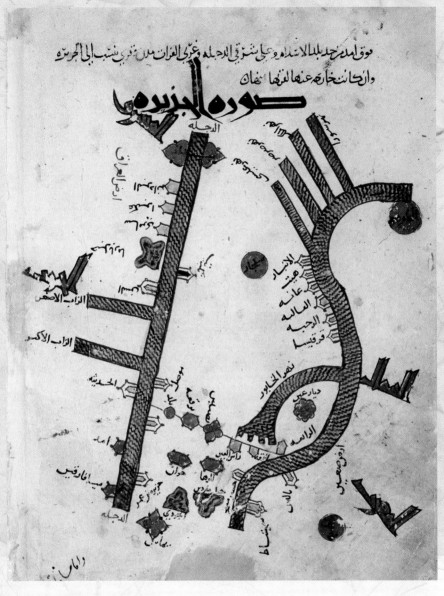

Created around the eleventh century AD, this map from a Syrian geographical atlas highlights the Tigris and Euphrates rivers, showing various settlements along their banks. These two rivers spurred the development of the Fertile Crescent, where the first civilizations of the Middle East emerged. Baghdad's location between them made the city a hub of the region in al-Khwarizmi's time.

these scholars, a wealth of knowledge from other cultures was translated and preserved.

THE ROOTS OF THE MUSLIM EMPIRE

The rise of the Muslim Empire can be traced to the prophet Muhammad, who was born in Mecca (or Makkah) in present-day Saudi Arabia in AD 570. Muslims believe that around 610, he was visited by the archangel Gabriel. Gabriel declared him a prophet of God, or Allah, and more visits followed. Encouraged by his wife and uncle, Muhammad began preaching the messages revealed to him, which were later collected in the Qur'an (or Koran). Few of Mecca's residents were willing to believe Muhammad. In 622, he was forced to flee to Medina (or Madinah, in present-day Saudi Arabia), an important event in Islamic history known as the Hijra (flight). There he made many converts and gained considerable political and religious authority. In the following years, Muhammad and his followers conquered Mecca and surrounding areas, making Muhammad the most powerful ruler in Arabia. He granted religious freedom to Christians and Jews as fellow "peoples of the Book" whose religious beliefs were considered close to that of Islam. He also preached against social distinctions based on race or social class.

Muhammad died suddenly in 632. After some disagreement among his followers, his close friend and father-in-law Abu

This sixteenth-century illustration from *Siyar-I Nabi* (The Life of the Prophet Muhammad) shows archangel Gabriel making one of his many visits to Muhammad. The manuscript was written around 1388 by Mustafa Darir, a blind Turkish poet, on a commission from Sultan Berkuk, the ruler of Cairo. Ottoman Sultan Murad III had the work illustrated in 1594.

Bakr was designated the first caliph, or successor to the Muslim-controlled territory. A chaotic period followed as various groups claiming the right to rule struggled for control. The Umayyad dynasty seized control in 661. At this time, the caliphate's borders included all of the Arabian Peninsula and North Africa. The Umayyads shifted the capital from Medina to Damascus, in present-day Syria, and began expanding their empire. By the early eighth century, the Muslim Empire extended well into central Asia and India. It conquered Turkey and Spain by 715, giving the Umayyads virtually complete control over the Mediterranean Sea.

Following the example set by Muhammad, the caliphs encouraged a degree of religious tolerance. Non-Muslims were allowed to worship as they chose and go about their business in complete freedom as long as they paid a tax and promised not to carry weapons. At first, these freedoms were offered only to Christians and Jews, but as the Muslim Empire conquered parts of India and the remnants of the Persian Empire, these freedoms were also extended to Hindus, Zoroastrians, and other religious groups as well. Nevertheless, non-Muslims were often persecuted by regional officials or blocked from holding government office. Though Muslim rule was a welcome change in regions where religious persecution was common, non-Muslims still found greater upward social mobility once they converted to Islam.

THE ABBASID DYNASTY AND THE FOUNDING OF BAGHDAD

Many Muslims grew discontented with the Umayyad dynasty, as the clan kept political offices in the hands of a few upper-class families from Mecca and Medina and began taxing Muslim lands. Most of the opposition originated in Persia, where many resented the Arab dominance of the region. They rallied behind the Abbasid clan, which claimed descent from Muhammad's uncle Abbas. The Abbasids revolted against the Umayyads in 749, killing the caliph.

This illustration from an eighteenth-century Persian manuscript shows two scenes from Abu al-Abbas al-Saffah's first sermon, after his ascendancy to the caliphate in the wake of the Abbasid overthrow of the Umayyad dynasty. The first scene shows people pledging their allegiance to al-Saffah. In the second scene, the new caliph is depicted at the top of the pulpit and talking to his uncle Abdullah. Abu Salama, a key warrior in the Umayyad overthrow, is shown at the foot of the pulpit.

The chief of the Abbasid clan, Abu al-Abbas al-Saffah, declared himself caliph in 749. He ruled as Amir al-Mu'minin, meaning "Commander of the Faithful." The caliph's brother, Abu Jafar al-Mansur began construction of the Abbasid's capital at Baghdad later that year. He chose a spot on the Tigris River not far from the Euphrates River. An extensive system of canals linked the city to a vast network of trade routes and irrigated the surrounding farmland. Trade routes connected the new city to Syria, Persia, Egypt, and beyond. Known as the "City of Peace," Baghdad grew into one of the world's wealthiest and most spectacular cities during the years of Abbasid rule.

Al-Mansur designed Baghdad to serve as the heart of the Muslim Empire. High walls bristling with towers and a deep moat protected the circular city, while four gates opened in the directions of Syria, the province of Khurasan, and the cities Basra and Kufa. By tradition, the city was also designed to set the caliph apart from its residents. An imperial complex, Dar al-Khalifa, formed the city's heart. It was dominated by a large mosque and a magnificent palace. The city's markets and residences all lay outside of the palace.

Under Abbasid rule, Baghdad grew into one of history's great cultural centers. The city and the caliphate experienced one of its richest periods of growth during the reign of Caliph Harun al-Rashid, the fifth caliph of the Abbasid dynasty. A skilled warrior, he led many military campaigns throughout

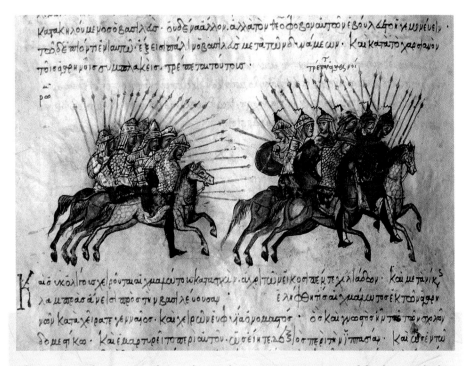

Between the seventh and ninth centuries, many Muslim caliphs invaded Byzantine territories with varying degrees of success. This miniature from John Scylitzes's *Chronicle* depicts a battle between Arab and Byzantine cavalries in 842. By then, the Arabs no longer posed a significant threat to the Byzantine Empire.

Asia. Harun al-Rashid expanded the empire as far as the Bosporus Strait and forced the Byzantine capital of Constantinople to pay tribute. As he aged, he turned his attention to diplomacy, maintaining diplomatic ties with China and the European emperor Charlemagne. At home, Baghdad's population soared as people of all races and beliefs flocked to the city. Muslims, Jews, Christians, Zoroastrians, pagans, and others mingled peacefully in Baghdad. However, civil unrest in present-day Syria and Iran brought about by abusive government officials forced Harun al-Rashid to spend a great deal of time living away from the capital.

Harun al-Rashid was a major patron of the arts. Under his rule, Muslim scholars began studying the arts and sciences of other societies, assimilating Greek and Indian knowledge into Arabic culture. A poet and scholar himself, he encouraged these arts by inviting a wide range of artists, musicians, and scholars to his palace and treating them with great respect. Many of these artists and scholars came from neighboring countries, bringing new knowledge to Harun al-Rashid's court.

When Harun al-Rashid died in 809, his son Muhammad ibn Harun al-Amin briefly became caliph before his death in 813. Harun al-Rashid's other son, Abu Jafar al-Mamun ibn Harun immediately became the seventh Abbasid caliph.

This gold dinar was issued in Baghdad during the reign of Harun al-Rashid, when Muslim coins began to make their way into Europe as a result of Harun al-Rashid exchanging ambassadors with King Charlemagne. It bears the name Musa (for the governor and finance director) at the base of the reverse area.

During his reign, the caliphate absorbed Afghanistan, the mountains of Persia, and parts of present-day Turkistan. After watching his father deal with numerous revolts throughout his empire, al-Mamun centralized the caliphate's power in Baghdad and limited the influence of regional governors. He also began a program that he called the *mihna*, or inquisition. The mihna was intended to guarantee the loyalty of al-Mamun's subjects and advisers through a series of questions relating to theology, faith, and loyalty. Punishments for failing the tests were harsh, and failure could even result in death.

Despite the harshness of the mihna, al-Mamun's legacy was shaped mostly through his dedication to scholarship. Like Harun al-Rashid, al-Mamun was a scholar and a great patron of artists. He founded an institution for scholars called the Bayt al-Hikma, or House of Wisdom. Through the House of Wisdom, al-Mamun encouraged the growth of knowledge in alchemy, mathematics, physics, astronomy, geography, and other fields. The scholars of the House of Wisdom were instrumental in translating scientific texts from various cultures, such as ancient Greece and India, into Arabic and preserving them for future generations.

Baghdad grew and prospered under al-Mamun's rule. Wealth flowed into the city as caravans and barges on the Tigris and Euphrates rivers continued to transport goods throughout the ever-expanding empire. Craftsmen, traders, and scholars seeking their fortunes flocked to the city. A cultural renaissance inspired by the work of the House of Wisdom was well under way, making Baghdad one of the most scientifically advanced cities of the era.

Al-Mamun left a mixed legacy for his heirs upon his death in 833. The scholastic work carried out by the House of Wisdom and Baghdad's growth brought learning and prosperity to the Muslim Empire. However, the mihna and al-Mamun's attempts to further centralize power only destabilized the Muslim Empire, as the subjects stopped trusting the caliphs and began directing their loyalty toward regional officials.

Al-Mamun's half-brother, Abu Ishaq al-Mutasim ibn Harun, ruled as caliph from 833 to 842. During his reign, the caliphate began relying on armies of Turkish slave-soldiers called mamluks to keep order. In 836, a garrison of mamluks incited a massive riot in Baghdad, forcing al-Mutasim to move the capital to the city of Samarra. Al-Mutasim's son, al-Wathiq ibn Mutasim, succeeded him and ruled until 847. Al-Mutasim and al-Wathiq continued to support the House of Wisdom, which remained in Baghdad. Al-Wathiq himself was an accomplished musician and composed more than 100 songs.

Al-Wathiq's brother, al-Mutawakkil Ala Allah Jafar bin al-Mutasim, inherited the caliphate. Al-Mutawakkil discontinued the mihna in 848, but he persecuted many of the religious minorities living in the Muslim Empire. Minority sects within Islam were repressed, as were Christians, Jews, and other minorities.

Al-Mutawakkil was less interested in learning or art than was his brother and his father. Consequently, the House of Wisdom declined rapidly during his rule. He did, however, have a keen eye for beauty and an interest in buildings. During his lifetime, his builders completed at least twenty new palaces and the Great Mosque of Samarra, known for its spiral minaret.

Al-Mutawakkil was assassinated in 861, after which the Abbasid dynasty declined rapidly. Regional governors began splitting away from the Muslim Empire, making use of dissatisfied mamluk forces to drive their rebellions. The capital was reestablished in Baghdad in 892, a move meant to symbolize the return of Abbasid dominance, but the city had also declined. Mongol forces put an end to Abbasid power in 1258, when they looted Baghdad and killed the caliph and hundreds of thousands of people.

THE PRESERVATION OF KNOWLEDGE

The Muslim Empire was vast in both geographical scale and in cultural diversity. Many different cultures and traditions were allowed to survive within its boundaries under the rule of the caliphs. The caliphate's encouragement of learning

This fourteenth-century illuminated manuscript page portrays the Mongol army crossing the Tigris River in its conquest of Baghdad in 1258. With this conquest the Mongols had occupied most of the former Muslim Empire. Hulagu, the victorious army commander and brother to the Mongol Khan (king), ruled over the region as Il-Khan (the lesser king) until 1265, thereby beginning the Ilkhanid period in Islamic history. In 1295, Ghazan, the ruling Il-Khan, converted to Islam, contributed to the translation and preservation of a great deal of knowledge from these various cultures.

Upon the foundation of the Muslim Empire, the earliest conquests made by early Muslims were of the regions surrounding the valleys of the Nile, the Tigris, and the Euphrates rivers. These lands had been settled for thousands of years and were home to advanced cultures. Some of these regions, particularly in Egypt, had been occupied by the Roman Empire before its collapse. During the years of Roman rule, scholars in Egypt studied the science and philosophy of the ancient Greeks. The conquering Arabs were a literate people, and they were extremely impressed by the information they gained from the Egyptians. The caliphs, particularly members of the Abbasid dynasty in Baghdad, actively sought to expand their knowledge and began encouraging scholars from other parts of the world to join their courts.

In the Islamic tradition, scholarship and knowledge was spread through a system of religious and legal schools called madrassas. Often associated with local mosques, these schools focused on religious and philosophical instruction throughout the Muslim Empire. Students of the madrassas learned to read, write, and do basic mathematics. Most of their instruction centered around the Qur'an. Instructors within the madrassas taught their students how to interpret the Qur'an's words. Accomplished students of

مقالها لقفخ الاسنابه امبيبه علعه نه نه اليخه امام هتفخ نه وت تسابه هتبابه

كج ع اليـ ـا لقـة لسـحك هذ انن لخن نسى اسه البه الهـ السه امس ع بح

اطه ان نا نفي نوى ليعا الجنخ نفى نغ نقا د هقيا اله لنحبا مقوله اله الحبه

لم سله نه ديتا تسكه نقام حرلقه نه ليا خفا حزا خه نقه لقه نفه كبيث
ك فه نفه نفه لقه اع ليا خفا خه نقه لقه نفه كبيث

the madrassas often made their way to Baghdad, where some found places within the House of Wisdom.

One of the primary goals of the House of Wisdom was the translation of classic texts from all over the known world into Arabic. Many of the manuscripts came from ancient Greece, while others came from India. The translations were stored in the library of the House of Wisdom along with records of the scientific discoveries made by Muslim scientists. All of these translations, documents, and records were easily accessible to other scholars.

In 751, paper manufactured from rags or tree bark was introduced to the Muslim Empire from China. Earlier forms of writing material, such as papyrus made from woven reeds or vellum made from calf skin, were costly to produce and purchase. By 793, a facility had been built in Baghdad for manufacturing paper. Scholars were thankful to have access to an inexpensive writing material, which helped them increase their written output.

The vast number of texts translated and preserved by the House of Wisdom allowed Muslim scholars and scientists access to information gathered in distant places and

This thirteenth-century miniature painting from Maqamat (Assemblies) by al-Hariri of Basrah portrays the interior of a mosque where it appears that a group of men are receiving religious instruction. In addition to being places of prayer, mosques have been central to the spread of education since as early as 653.

A Thousand and One Nights

Shortly before the middle of the tenth century, a Baghdad scholar named al-Jahshiyari compiled tales for what would later become the classic *A Thousand and One Nights (Alf Laylah wa-Laylah)*. In the story, the queen Scheherazade is condemned to die by her husband, the sultan Shahryar. The night before her execution, she tells a story to her sister so that the sultan will overhear. She stops before she finishes the tale, and the curious sultan allows her to live another day so that she can tell the rest the next night. Scheherazade repeats this pattern for 1,001 nights, until the sultan relents and removes the death sentence.

Al-Jahshiyari based his work on an old Persian text called *A Thousand Tales (Hazar Afsana)*, which consisted of stories originating in ancient India. *A Thousand Tales* provided the work's structure and many of the character names, including Scheherazade. He incorporated anecdotes and folktales from the oral folk traditions of Persia, Egypt, and Arabia. Historical figures were also added to the work. In particular, the court of Caliph Harun al-Rashid was used as the setting for many humorous escapades and romances. Other writers continued adding tales to *A Thousand and One Nights* until it reached its present form in the late fifteenth century. Today it remains widely popular due to its exotic background and the appeal of characters such as Ali Baba, Aladdin, and Sinbad the Sailor, which were added later.

from various time periods. They could then combine and expand on these ideas in their own texts, making new discoveries as they progressed in their studies. Their translations and new discoveries also spread throughout the Muslim Empire, ending up in provincial libraries and schools through the empire's vast trade network. Many of the works that survived the end of the Abbasid dynasty later helped to reawaken Europe's interest in learning. Translated from Arabic into Latin or Greek, they formed the basis for the European Renaissance and the core of Europe's scientific, philosophical, and literary growth.

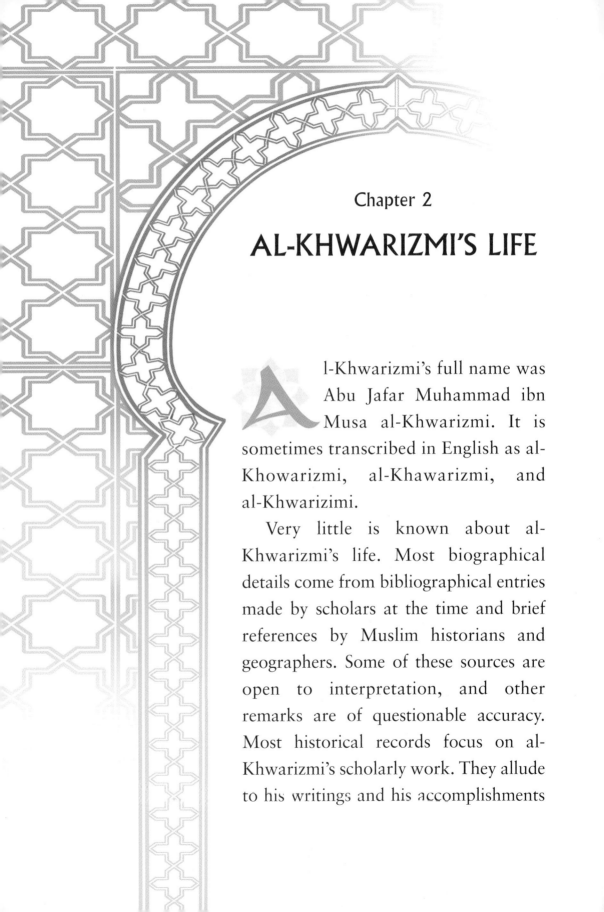

Chapter 2

AL-KHWARIZMI'S LIFE

Al-Khwarizmi's full name was Abu Jafar Muhammad ibn Musa al-Khwarizmi. It is sometimes transcribed in English as al-Khowarizmi, al-Khawarizmi, and al-Khwarizimi.

Very little is known about al-Khwarizmi's life. Most biographical details come from bibliographical entries made by scholars at the time and brief references by Muslim historians and geographers. Some of these sources are open to interpretation, and other remarks are of questionable accuracy. Most historical records focus on al-Khwarizmi's scholarly work. They allude to his writings and his accomplishments

This statue of al-Khwarizmi is located outside the Mohammed Amin Khan Madrassa (school) in Khiva, Uzbekistan, where the scholar was born or his family originated. The site is one of the most impressive buildings in Uzbekistan and, as such, a popular tourist attraction. Al-Khwarizmi's statue there evidences the esteem in which he is held in Uzbekistan.

as a mathematician, astronomer, and geographer. Historians make almost no mention of his personal life.

The name al-Khwarizmi indicates that he came from Khwarizm, or Khorezm, a region in central Asia south of the Aral Sea. Khwarizm was once a thriving kingdom of antiquity. It later became a province of the Persian Empire, and the region fell under control of the Muslim rulers in 680. Today, Khwarizm is the city of Khiva in Uzbekistan.

The historian G. J. Toomer hypothesizes in *The Dictionary of Scientific Biography*, however, that it was actually al-Khwarizmi's family that originally came from Khwarizm, not al-Khwarizmi himself. Other historians dispute Toomer's theory. Toomer cites the historian al-Tabari (838–923) as a source, but it is likely that Toomer simply misinterpreted an error in a copy of al-Tabari's manuscript. Uzbekistan proudly counts al-Khwarizmi as one of the nation's great historical figures.

The exact year of al-Khwarizmi's birth is also not known. He was probably born around 780, shortly before Harun al-Rashid became caliph.

THE HOUSE OF WISDOM

Al-Khwarizmi was appointed a member of the House of Wisdom by Caliph al-Mamun, who reigned from 813 to 833.

ПОЧТА ❋❋ СССР ❋ 1983

1200 ЛЕТ МУХАММЕД аль-ХОРЕЗМИ

The Union of Soviet Socialist Republics (USSR) issued this four-kopeck stamp in 1983 to commemorate the 1200th anniversary of al-Khwarizmi's birth. The portrait is really a speculative depiction of the great scholar, as there is no evidence of what he actually looked like.

He dedicated two of his early works, *Kitab al-Jabr wal-Muqabala* and *Zij*, which is a treatise on astronomy, to the caliph, who was a great patron of science and learning. Al-Mamun was succeeded by his brother al-Mutasim, who

The House of Wisdom was a research academy that attracted some of the brightest minds of ninth-century Arabia. With the support of al-Mamun, who founded the institution around 830, it quickly became the intellectual hub of Baghdad, which was itself one of the most important centers for scientific and philosophical inquiry in the Muslim Empire for centuries. This fourteenth-century painting portrays a discussion among scholars in the House of Wisdom.

reigned from 833 to 842, and later al-Mutasim's elder son, al-Wathiq, who reigned from 842 to 847. The Abbasid dynasty declined under al-Wathiq's brother al-Mutawakkil, who reigned from 847 to 861. Al-Khwarizmi served under all of these caliphs. In the introduction to his work on algebra

(*Kitab al-Jabr wal-Muqabala*), al-Khwarizmi extravagantly thanks and praises al-Mamun:

> That fondness for science, by which God has distinguished the IMAN AL MAMUN, the Commander of the Faithful (besides the caliphate which He has vouchsafed unto him by lawful succession, in the robe of which He has invested him, and with the honors of which He has adorned him), that affability and condescension which he shows to the learned, that promptitude with which he protects and supports them in the elucidation of obscurities and in the removal of difficulties—has encouraged me to compose a short work.

There is no evidence that al-Khwarizmi's loyalty to the caliphs ever wavered.

Al-Khwarizmi is considered by many to have been the greatest scholar of his day. In his book *Introduction to the History of Science*, historian George Sarton refers to the first half of the ninth century as "the time of al-Khwarizmi." (According to Sarton, the second half of the eighth century was "the time of Jabar ibn Haiyan," an alchemist, and the second half of the ninth century was "the time of al-Razi," who is best remembered as a physician.) Baghdad during this period was one of the great intellectual centers of the world, and many of al-Khwarizmi's colleagues in the House of Wisdom are known for significant

The son of a governor, al-Kindi was one of the most influential scholars of the ninth century. In addition to overseeing the translation of important Greek works at the House of Wisdom, he was an original philosopher who was also skilled in medicine, music, mathematics, and geography. He is widely regarded as the father of Arab philosophy.

contributions to science and philosophy.

One of al-Khwarizmi's contemporaries at the House of Wisdom, Abu Yusuf Yaqub ibn Ishaq al-Sabah al-Kindi, (circa 801–873), is known as the first great Muslim philosopher. Al-Kindi studied the earliest Arabic translations of Aristotle (384–332 BC), and his own philosophy was heavily influenced by Aristotle's writings and Neo-platonism, a reinterpretation of Plato (ca. 427–347 BC). He contended in his philosophical works that the conclusions of religion and philosophy could be reconciled, but that philosophy and reason were inferior to the divine insight of religion. His works deal with a variety of subjects and include an important treatise on optics, the first known Muslim discussion of music, and writings on medicine and physics. Like al-Khwarizmi, al-Kindi was also a mathematician and astronomer. Al-Kindi was persecuted late in his career by Caliph al-Mutawakkil, who maintained a traditional Sunni interpretation of Islam.

Al-Khwarizmi also worked at the House of Wisdom at the same time as the three Banu Musa brothers, Jafar Muhammad, al-Hasan, and Ahmad. "Banu Musa" means "the sons of Musa." Their father, Musa ibn Shakir, was a former robber who became an able astrologer later in his life. The brothers are best remembered for their work in geometry, but Ahmad was also interested in mechanics. In *Kitab al-Hiyal* (Book of Ingenious Devices), he describes a contraption that would deliver hot and cold water, devices for digging wells, and a lamp with a self-trimming wick. Along with al-Khwarizmi, the Banu Musa brothers were the leading researchers at the House of Wisdom. They also supervised the translators working at the House of Wisdom and led astronomical observations.

During al-Mamun's reign, astronomers at the House of Wisdom undertook the operation of measuring a terrestrial degree. A terrestrial degree is the length on land of one degree of arc in the sky. With this information, they could determine the size of Earth. They computed the length of a terrestrial degree to be 56⅔ Arabic miles (roughly 6,473 feet [1,973 meters]), a distance we now know to be in error by about 2,877 feet (877 m). According to this figure, the earth would be about 20,400 miles (32,831 kilometers) in circumference and 6,500 miles (10,461 km) in diameter. In reality, Earth has a circumference of 24,902 miles (40,076 km) and a diameter

This illustration from *Shahinshahnama* (Book of the King of Kings), a sixteenth-century Turkish manuscript, shows astronomers at work in an Istanbul observatory, using a range of observational and measuring instruments. Many of the advances in astronomy between the eighth and sixteenth centuries took place within the Muslim Empire.

of 7,900 miles (12,714 km) at the equator. The Banu Musa brothers and al-Khwarizmi almost certainly participated in the project. However, this indicates a belief in the roundness of the earth.

A SCHOLAR OF BAGHDAD

After becoming a member of the House of Wisdom, al-Khwarizmi lived and worked in Baghdad for the rest of his life. Historical records leave almost no clues about his daily activities, travel, family and friends, or reaction to the reception of his work.

Historians have speculated on al-Khwarizmi's native language. Since he was born in a former Persian province, he may have spoken the Persian language. It is also possible that he spoke Khwarezmian, a language of the region that is now extinct. Although the caliph's court welcomed non-Muslim scientists, they had a lower status than Muslims. Nonbelievers were not free to openly express ideas contrary to orthodox Islam. In his book *The Universal History of Numbers*, the scholar Georges Ifrah quotes al-Biruni, a native of Khwarizm, on a Muslim ruler's repression of Khwarizm's culture.

Thus Qutaybah did away with those who knew the script of Khwarizm, who understood the country's traditions and taught the knowledge of its inhabitants; he submitted them to tortures so that they were wrapped up in shadows and no one could know (even in Khwarizm) what had (preceded) or followed the birth of Islam.

Qutaybah ibn Muslim was the governor of the province of Khorasan and a conqueror who greatly expanded the Muslim Empire to the west during the early eighth century.

Al-Biruni's testimony brings up the question of al-Khwarizmi's religion. The historian al-Tabari referred to al-Khwarizmi in one instance as "al-Majusi" in his *Tarikh ur-Rusul wal-Muluk* (History of the Prophets and Kings), often referred to simply as his *Annals*. In this instance, "al-Majusi," which means "magus" or "magician,"was used as an ethnic designation for a practicing Zoroastrian or some-one whose ancestors were Zoroastrian. Al-Khwarizmi reveals very little personal information in his writings. He did, however, offer thanks to God in the introduction to his work on algebra.

Prais'd be God for his bounty towards those who deserve it by their virtuous acts . . . He sent MOHAMMED (on whom may the blessing of God repose!) with the mission of a prophet, long after any messenger from above had appeared, when jus-tice had fallen into neglect, and when the true way of life was sought for in vain. Through him he was cured of blindness, and saved through him from perdition, and increased through him what before was small, and collected through him what before was scattered. Praised be God our Lord! and may his glory increase, and may all his names be hallowed—besides

Zoroastrianism

Al-Khwarizmi was not a Zoroastrian himself, but this ancient religion was still widely practiced during the years of the Abbasid dynasty. Zoroastrianism is a religion named for its founder, the prophet Zoroaster, who likely lived in ancient Persia during the seventh century BC. Virtually nothing is known about his life, but he established the core teachings of his faith in a collection of psalms called the Gathas. Zoroastrianism is based on the worship of Ahura Mazda, the Lord Wisdom. Zoroastrians believe that all of the good in the universe comes from Ahura Mazda's creative force, called Spenta Mainyu. Spenta Mainyu is assisted by six entities: Good Mind, Truth, Health, Life, Power, and Devotion. Spenta Mainyu's twin and opposite, Angra Mainyu, is the source of all evil. Whereas Spenta Mainyu represents truth, Angra Mainyu represents lies, or falseness. Upon death, people who follow truth and the way of Spenta Mainyu will cross over to paradise, while followers of lies and Angra Mainyu are sent to a fiery underworld.

Zoroastrianism eventually spread throughout Asia, but Persia remained the religion's stronghold for many centuries. Many of the emperors of ancient Persia were Zoroastrians, starting with Darius I, who ruled from 521 to 486 BC. When the Sassanid dynasty took the Persian throne in AD 224, it made Zoroastrianism Persia's state religion. The Muslim conquest of Persia in the seventh century ended Zoroastrian dominance, and the religion declined as the region's population converted to Islam. Today, there are an estimated 250,000 Zoroastrians worldwide, most of whom live around Bombay, India. Substantial numbers of Zoroastrians live in Iran and the United States.

Carved into a cliff in Naqsh-iRustam, Iran, this relief depicts Ardashir I, founder of the Sassanid Empire in Persia in the third century AD, receiving a crown from the Zoroastrian god Ahura Mazda. Upon coming to power, Ardashir I made Zoroastrianism the state-sanctioned religion, declaring that his rule was the will of God.

whom there is no God; and may his benediction rest on MOHAMMED the Prophet and on his descendants!

Al-Khwarizmi's words make it clear that he was a pious Muslim. It is possible that al-Tabari meant that al-Khwarizmi's family was once Zoroastrian, or that al-Khwarizmi was

Zoroastrian when he was younger. If he did convert to Islam from Zoroastrianism, the move would have greatly benefitted his position at court.

Historical records suggest that in 842, Caliph al-Wathiq may have sent al-Khwarizmi to the northern Caucasus mountain region to meet with the chief of the Khazars. The Khazars were an ancient people who controlled trade between the Caspian Sea and the Black Sea. It is possible, however, that it was the Banu Musa brother Jafar Muhammad ibn Musa ibn Shakir who traveled to the Caucasus, not al-Khwarizmi. Similarly, it was probably the Banu Musa brother Jafar Muhammad who made an expedition to Greece to investigate the tomb of the Seven Sleepers of Ephesus. According to legend, the sleepers were seven Christian youths who took refuge in a cave from the religious persecution of the Roman emperor Decius. The emperor had the cave boarded up, but the Seven Sleepers woke from a sleep 200 years later. Their existence reaffirmed the faith of Emperor Theodosius II, and they returned to sleep in the cave until the Day of Judgment. The legend, thought to be of Syrian origin, was popular among both Muslims and Christians. An Islamic version of the story is found in the Qur'an's Surat al-Kahf, or "Chapter of the Cave." The historian and scientist al-Biruni wrote that in the ninth century, corpses of monks believed to have been the Seven Sleepers were displayed in a cave. Even though al-Khwarizmi may not have traveled to the Caucasus or to

Greece, these accounts give an idea of some of the more exceptional duties of the scholars of the House of Wisdom.

The last known historical reference to al-Khwarizmi is in al-Tabari's *Annals*. He was among a group of astronomers who attended Caliph al-Wathiq as he lay on his deathbed in 847. They consulted the stars and assured him that he would reign for fifty more years. Nonetheless, the caliph died ten days later.

If al-Tabari was correct in naming al-Khwarizmi as one of the astronomers present, he would have been nearly seventy years old. Most sources list "about 850" as the year of his death.

AL-KHWARIZMI'S WRITINGS

Al-Khwarizmi wrote a number of groundbreaking works during his long career.

His most famous work, of course, is his *Kitab al-Jabr wal-Muqabala*, which laid the foundations for modern algebra. He completed both this work and *Zij*, his astronomical treatise, during al-Mamun's reign from 813 to 833.

Al-Khwarizmi included this map of the island of Yaqut (most likely, present-day Sri Lanka) in his *Kitab Surat al-Ard* (*Geography* or "Book of the form of the earth"). The line at right represents the equator.

عنه احمل نقط كنط كرم الاقرب لاني رو اول رحل المشوق رح اقصا الصفين

لنذكرك السماك

وحبل محط ط ا ده ا النقوث سندى مرطول قس ه وعض مك ه وطول ط ا ج ح ح ط ه
على اسفى نرسمبلر الى عرض ه وطول مع ه ومن نقط المرا المط ه عندعرض
ده وطول نقط ه وطط ده الى عرض ك وطول فعح مر خط الحروب على وهه
الصط م ى الحل على طول فعح ا حنى سهل الى الخط الاسق مرسد ا الى الطول بعوك
وكور العوص ط ه ح ط ه الاسق ه ا مرسد ا الى الطول فعح ه ماس لخط الاسق
مر كن على نقط الطول الى الرصد الى العص م ا لعلم ا اول ه مرسد ا الى الرصد
العوص طك ك والطول فعك مرسلر الى الرصد الطول فعح ه والعوص ك ه
ولونه احمر بوس ف ومسد الحل الى المشوق ومر حول الجل وهده صورته

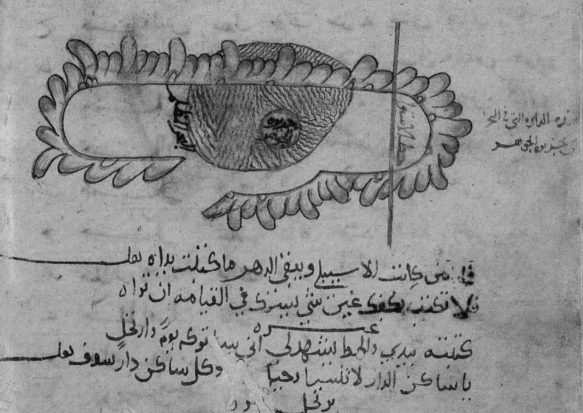

في منى كانت الاسبيلي ويبقى الدهر ماكنت بداه بعلا
الا تكن يكفك عين سى يسبرك في القيامه ان نواه
كينته مدرب الخط السهلى انى بسو توك يوم وارحل
يا ساكن الدار لا تنسبا وحيا وكل ساكن دار سوف نرحل بعلا

د د

Of his other works, only *Istikhraj Ta'rikh al-Yahud* (About the Jewish Calendar), a short work on Jewish dating systems, can be dated. Calculations within the text mention that al-Khwarizmi worked on it during 823 and 824. His work on Hindi numerals, the basis for the Arabic system of numbers we use today, was composed sometime after *Kitab al-Jabr wal-Muqabala*. He wrote *Kitab al-Ta'rikh* (Chronicle), a history account based on astrology, sometime after 826. His other major work was his *Geography (Kitab Surat al-Ard,* which translates as "Book of the Form of the Earth").

Al-Khwarizmi wrote his works in Arabic. During the golden age of Islam, Arabic was nearly the universal language of the intellectual world. As Muslim scientists absorbed knowledge from other cultures, the Arabic language had to incorporate new concepts. The Arabic vocabulary expanded, and existing words were adapted to new needs. The Arabic language became the best language of the time for expressing scientific thought.

Only a few of al-Khwarizmi's works have been preserved in their original Arabic. A couple exist in Latin translations. Some have been lost and are known only because of references in other sources from the time.

Al-Khwarizmi is primarily remembered today as a mathematician, but he was also an outstanding astronomer and geographer. It was quite common for

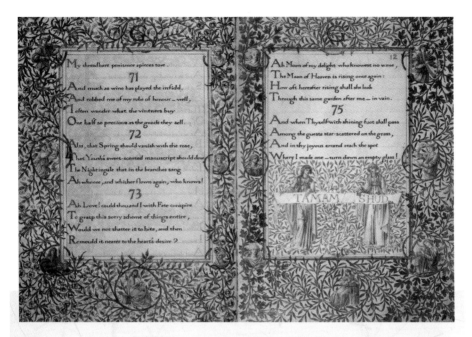

This is a page spread from a nineteenth-century English adaptation of Umar al-Khayyam's *Rubáiyát*, one of the most widely read literary classics. The son of a tentmaker who rose to become the chief astrologer to Persian sultan Malikshah Jalal al-Din, al-Khayyam wrote many influential texts on mathematics and physics.

scholars of his day to explore many fields of study. In addition, different areas of expertise were not as sharply differentiated as they are today. Most mathematicians, for example, also studied astronomy or astrology. Al-Khwarizmi's colleagues al-Kindi and the Banu Musa brothers explored a variety of subjects. Al-Farabi (ca. 870–950), for example, was an important philosopher, but he also studied mathematics, music, and medicine. The great scholar al-Biruni (973–1048) was a historian, mathematician, scientist, philosopher, and traveler.

One of the most famous figures of the golden age of Islam, Umar al-Khayyam (1048–1123), was a mathematician and astronomer as well as the author of the *Rubáiyát*, which means "quatrains." In one of the verses (translated by Edward Fitzgerald), al-Khayyam playfully refers to his work in reforming the Persian calendar.

Ah, but my Computations, People say,
Reduced the Year to better reckoning?—Nay
'Twas only striking from the Calendar
Unborn To-morrow, and dead Yesterday.

As a mathematician who studied algebra, al-Khayyam was undoubtedly quite familiar with al-Khwarizmi's work. In addition, both men studied and wrote about calendars.

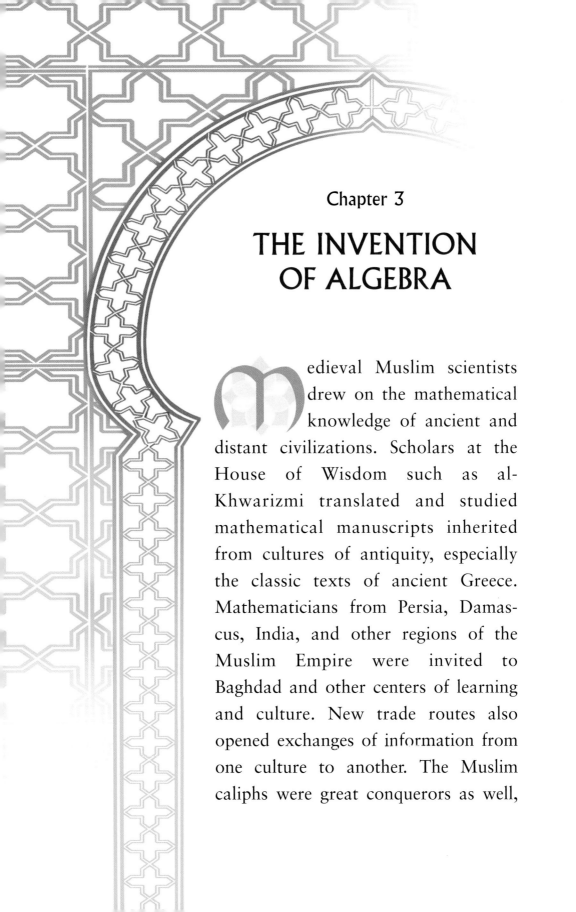

Chapter 3

THE INVENTION
OF ALGEBRA

edieval Muslim scientists drew on the mathematical knowledge of ancient and distant civilizations. Scholars at the House of Wisdom such as al-Khwarizmi translated and studied mathematical manuscripts inherited from cultures of antiquity, especially the classic texts of ancient Greece. Mathematicians from Persia, Damascus, India, and other regions of the Muslim Empire were invited to Baghdad and other centers of learning and culture. New trade routes also opened exchanges of information from one culture to another. The Muslim caliphs were great conquerors as well,

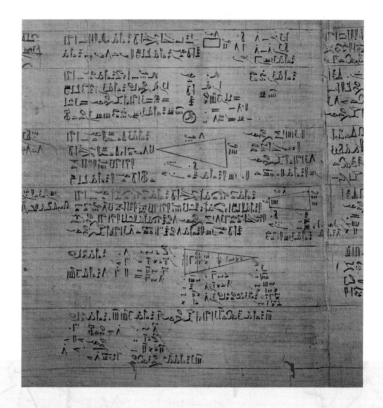

This Egyptian mathematical papyrus dates back to about 1650 BC. It was created by a scribe named Ahmes, who noted that he did not write the manuscript, but merely copied it from an earlier work that was written in 2000 BC. Much of our knowledge of mathematics in ancient Egypt comes from papyri such as this one.

and as they seized new territory, they also gained access to the closely guarded secrets of the societies they conquered.

Muslim mathematicians assimilated and systemized the mathematical scholarship of these various sources. In turn, they contributed greatly to the development of mathematics, especially to the branches of arithmetic, algebra, geometry, and trigonometry.

MATHEMATICS BEFORE THE RISE OF THE MUSLIM EMPIRE

As Georges Ifrah points out in his book *The Universal History of Numbers*, most human societies have developed some method of numerical notation. (He also notes that even some animals have an innate "sense of number.") The Egyptians and Babylonians were the first cultures to develop an organized system of mathematics.

The earliest existing Egyptian mathematical papyruses date from about 1750 BC. The Egyptians used a decimal system of numbering, meaning that numbers are expressed in powers of ten. Specific hieroglyphs represented 1, 10, 100, 1,000, 10,000, 100,000, and 1,000,000. The Egyptians also had a simplistic system for calculating fractions. Their mathematical processes involved little more than arithmetic and basic geometry necessary for calculations in agriculture, trade, and the construction of monuments such as the pyramids.

The Babylonians of Mesopotamia developed a more advanced system of mathematics as early as 1950 BC. Ancient

This Mesopotamian cuneiform tablet presents an accounting of goats and sheep. It dates back to around 2350 BC. Cuneiform script is one of the earliest known forms of writing.

cuneiform tablets show that they used a sexagesimal system of numbering—it was based on the number sixty rather than ten. Today, measurement of time is based on a sexagesimal system. (There are sixty seconds in a minute and sixty minutes in an hour).

The Babylonians made a significant mathematical achievement in establishing a place value system in their numbering. Today, our decimal system of numbers uses a place system with a ones place, a tens place, a hundreds place, and so on. The Babylonians had fifty-nine different roughly wedge-shaped numbers. (The Babylonians used symbols that resembled wedges or combinations of wedges to represent their numbers.) The number 60 was represented by the same symbol as the number 1, but it was moved over one place value. Babylonian mathematicians made advances in arithmetic, including long division and multiplication, fractions, and geometry. They were also familiar with some basic algebraic concepts.

This detail from Raphael's famous fresco *School of Athens* portrays Pythagoras with a young student. Although most known for the mathematical theorem that bears his name, Pythagoras also made important contributions to science, music, and astronomy. Although he produced no written works, he had a large following of students who advanced his teachings by word of mouth until eventually their successors wrote them down.

It was the Greeks who transformed mathematics from a practical calculating tool into a logical system. The Greeks drew on Egyptian and Babylonian knowledge, but they established abstract definitions, laws, and proofs for mathematical concepts. One of the first great Greek mathematicians was Pythagoras of Samos (592–496 BC), who lived during the sixth century BC. He believed that everything in the world could be understood through mathematics. He even believed there were numbers for such concepts as justice and the soul.

The most famous Greek mathematician was Euclid (325–265 BC), who taught at the famous school of Alexandria during the third century BC. He compiled Greek knowledge of geometry into a thirteen-volume work called *The Elements*. It is famous for its logic and clarity, and translations were used as a text in schools until the nineteenth century. After Euclid, mathematicians such as Archimedes (ca. 287–212 BC), Apollonius of Perga (ca. 262–190 BC), and Claudius Ptolemy (ca. AD 85–165) made further advances in geometry.

The Greeks used what is called an acrophonic system of numbers. Numbers were represented by the first letter of the Greek name for the number. The notation was very similar to the Egyptian hieroglyphic system.

Muslim scholars translated the texts of Aristotle, Euclid, Archimedes, Ptolemy, Apollonius, and other Greek mathematicians, as well as works from China, India, and ancient Babylonia. Persian, Sanskrit, Koptic, and Aramaic works were also translated and preserved. Muslim mathematicians wrote commentaries on these ancient and foreign texts, refined and expanded their mathematical knowledge, and built on each other's work. Copies of translations and original works by Muslim scholars were circulated to universities and libraries across the empire. After the decline of the Muslim Empire many of these manuscripts survived, especially in Spanish institutions.

Al-Khwarizmi represents both facets of Muslim scholarship. He made original contributions to mathematics and also worked to preserve and transmit mathematical knowledge from other cultures. His most famous work, the *Al-Jabr wal-Muqabala*, opened up a whole new discipline of mathematics. Al-Khwarizmi also wrote a treatise that introduced and explained Hindi numerals and methods of calculations.

AL–JABR WAL–MUQABALA

Modern algebra is the branch of mathematics in which numbers and other elements of equations can be represented by letters. Algebra provides a generalization of arithmetic. The equation $a + a = 2a$, for example, will be true for any number that the letter a might represent. Algebraic math problems often require that the student solve an equation by finding the value for an unknown variable, often x. In the equation $ax^2 + bx = c$, for example, a, b, and c are replaced with numbers. The value of x will depend on the values of a, b, and c, but the

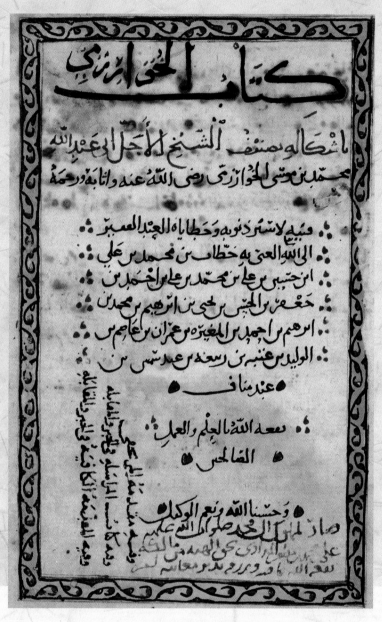

This is the frontispiece for al-Khwarizimi's original manuscript for *Kitab al Jabr wal-Muqabala.* In 1140, it was translated into Latin as *Liber Algebrae et Almucabala,* from which the English word "algebra" derives.

equation can always be solved by using the same mathematical processes.

Al-Khwarizmi did not set out to found a new branch of mathematics when he wrote *Al-Jabr wal-Muqabala*. In the introduction to the work, he declares his intent in very practical terms. He describes his text in this way:

A short work on Calculating by (the rules of) Completion and Reduction confining it to what is easiest and most useful in arithmetic, such as men constantly require in cases of inheritance, legacies, partition, law-suits, and trade, and in all their dealings with one another, or where the measuring of lands, the digging of canals, geometrical computation, and other objects of various sorts and kinds are concerned.

Al-Khwarizmi wanted his work to help people solve mathematical dilemmas in their everyday lives.

The full title is *Kitab al-Jabr wal-Muqabala*. "Kitab" merely means "the book of." "Al-Jabr" refers to the removal of negative terms from a mathematical equation. "Muqabala" means "reduction" or "balancing the equation to a simpler form." "Al-Jabr wal-Muqabala" as a whole has come to mean generally "the process of performing algebraic operations."

The book consists of three sections. The first part is the theoretical basis of what we now know as algebra. The second is concerned with mensuration, or the geometry of computing lengths, areas, and volumes. The final section is on legacies, and it deals with the mathematics of Islamic inheritance laws.

The first part begins by introducing the reader to numbers.

> When I consider what people generally want in calculating, I found that it always is a number. I also observed that every number is composed of units, and that any number may be divided into units. Moreover, I found that every number which may be expressed from one to ten, surpasses the preceding by one unit: afterwards the ten is doubled or tripled just as before the units were: thus arise twenty, thirty, etc. until a hundred: then the hundred is doubled and tripled in the same manner as the units and the tens, up to a thousand . . . so forth to the utmost limit of numeration.

Al-Khwarizmi uses no symbols or written equations throughout his work. Every mathematical process is expressed in words.

After introducing numbers, al-Khwarizmi moves on to the process of solving mathematical equations. He discusses both linear and quadratic equations, two types of basic algebraic equations. According to al-Khwarizmi, all linear and quadratic equations can be reduced to six forms:

(1) $ax^2 = bx$
(2) $ax^2 = b$
(3) $ax = b$

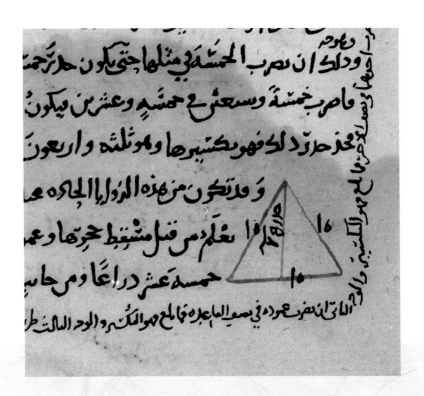

This is a part of a page from *Kitab al-Jabr wal-Muqabala*. Unlike modern algebra texts, the book is written in prose form, with no mathematical symbols.

(4) $ax^2 + bx = c$

(5) $ax^2\ 2 + c = bx$

(6) $ax^2 = bx + c$

The quantities a, b, and c represent known numbers. The unknown quantity is x. By using numbers in place of a, b, and c, the reader can use al-Khwarizmi's equations to find the numerical value for x.

These six equations are written in modern mathematical notation. Al-Khwarizmi describes the equations in words. For example, he states one problem in these terms:

A quantity: I multiplied a third of it and a *dirham* by a fourth of it and a dirham; it becomes twenty.

In modern notation, it is written $(x/3 + 1)(x/4 + 1) = 20$. A dirham is a type of coin, and al-Khwarizmi used it to signify a single numerical unit. He goes on to reduce and solve the equation. Here is the first step of the process:

Its computation is that you multiply a third of something by a fourth of something: it comes to a half of a sixth of a square. And you multiply a dirham by a third of something: it comes to a third of something; and [you multiply] a dirham by a fourth of something to get a fourth of something; and [you multiply] a dirham by a dirham to get a dirham . . .Thus its total, [namely] a half of a sixth of a square and third of something and a quarter of something and a dirham, is equal to twenty dirhams.

In modern notation, the equation he describes is $[x^2/12 + x/3 + x/4 + 1 = 20]$. Multiplying out mathematical expressions in this way is a basic process taught today in introductory algebra. Al-Khwarizmi goes on to further simplify the equation to solve for x.

One of al-Khwarizmi's great accomplishments in writing his *Al-Jabr wal-Muqabala* was the establishment of algebra as a separate branch of mathematics from geometry. Geometry had been known for millennia, and it was thoroughly refined by the Greeks. By contrast, many of al-Khwarizmi's algebraic concepts were original and new to the study of mathematics. Nevertheless, al-Khwarizmi did use geometrical proofs for the answers to some of his equations.

In one case, al-Khwarizmi poses this question to his readers:

For instance, "one square, and ten roots of the same, amount to thirty-nine dirhams"; that is to say, what must be the square which, when increased by ten of its own roots, amount to thirty-nine?

This can be put into modern notation: $x^2 + 10x = 39$. This is an example of a quadratic equation that follows the fourth form of his six types of equations. He then presents the solution:

You halve the number of the roots, which in the present instance yields five. This you multiply by itself; the product is twenty-five. Add this to thirty-nine; the sum is sixty-four.

The equations for these steps are $(x + 5)^2 = 39 + 25 = 64$.

Now take the root of this, which is eight, and subtract from it half the number of the roots, which is five; the remainder is three. This is the root of the square which you sought for; the square itself is nine.

Therefore, $x + 5 = \sqrt{64}$, and $x + 5 = 8$, so $x = 3$. Later in the section, al-Khwarizmi demonstrates the solution geometrically by describing a square, "the figure A B, each side of which may be considered as one of its roots." He shows how his algebraic solution can be proved by adding a narrow rectangle to each side of the square and then adding small squares at each corner. The algebraic process demonstrated by this proof is known as "completing the square."

Al-Khwarizmi ends the first part of his *Al-Jabr wal-Muqabala* with a short section titled "On Business Transactions." It deals with computing quantities, prices, and other practical transactions.

The second section of the work is on mensuration. It describes how to compute areas and volumes of various

As al-Khwarizmi noted in his groundbreaking work in algebra, his primary concern in writing the book was standardizing and simplifying methods of making the routine calculations that ordinary people encountered in their daily lives. Accordingly, the transactions of traders, such as the ones depicted weighing merchandise on this Egyptian manuscript page, would have received much of his consideration.

بِالْإِبْهَامِ وَالشَّهَادَةِ وَالْوُسْطَى وَذَلِكَ إِدْمَانُ

الْقُوَى وَعَلَيْكَ بِالْكَبَّادِ وَهَذَا صِفَةُ نَصْبِ الْقَنْدَافِ

بِ وَهَلْ صِفَةُ الْوَزْنِ وَالْإِدْمَانُ وَعَلَيْكَ بِالْكَبَّ

الْأَوْقَاتِ

shapes and solids. Al-Khwarizmi gives equations for finding the area and circumference of a circle, for example, and for computing the volumes of cones, pyramids, and truncated pyramids. At one point, he gives a fairly accurate estimate of the number π (pi). Al-Khwarizmi also presents the famous Pythagorean theorem established by the Greeks: $[a^2 + b^2 = c^2]$. The theorem states that for a right triangle (a triangle with one right angle), the square of the hypoteneuse c (the long side) is equal to the sum of the squares of the two short sides a and b. Al-Khwarizmi's proof of the theorem is different than the proof presented in Euclid's *Elements*, however. This indicates that even if al-Khwarizmi was familiar with the *Elements*, it was not one of his main sources for background research on *Al-Jabr wal-Muqabala*.

The third and longest part deals with the mathematics of legacies. It consists of problems and solutions involving inheritance according to Islamic laws. The mathematics in this section are fairly simple, but the problems require expertise on the complex Islamic system of inheritance. Under this system, people inherited fixed ratios of the deceased's property based on their relationship with the deceased.

TREATISE ON HINDI NUMERALS

Al-Khwarizmi's treatise on Hindi numerals has been lost. Historians are not even completely sure of the exact title. It is often referred to as *Kitab al Jami' wa'l Tafriq bi-Hisab al-Hind* (Indian Technique of Addition and Subtraction), but it could also have been something like *Kitab Hisab al-Adad al-Hindi* (Treatise on Calculation with the Hindi Numerals). Both possible versions of the title convey al-Khwarizmi's intent in writing this work. It was his introduction of Hindi numbers and methods of calculation to the Islamic intellectual world.

Historians have long debated the precise origin of the Arabic numerals that we use today. It is true that Muslim texts introduced these numerals to the Western world, but they were not invented by Muslim mathematicians. In his book *The Universal History of Numbers*, Georges Ifrah gives convincing evidence that the system of numbers we use today originated in India centuries before the rise of the Muslim Empire. He references the scholar al-Biruni as one of his sources. Al-Biruni lived in India for many years and wrote about Indian mathematics and science in many of his books.

The Indians developed the numbers 1 to 9 and 0, and they established the decimal place value system. Some historians have theorized that their place value system may have been influenced by the Babylonian sexagesimal place value system. One fundamental breakthrough in Indian mathematics was its use of zero as a placeholder. The modern number fifty, for example, contains a five in the tens place and a zero in the ones place. The zero is the placeholder that

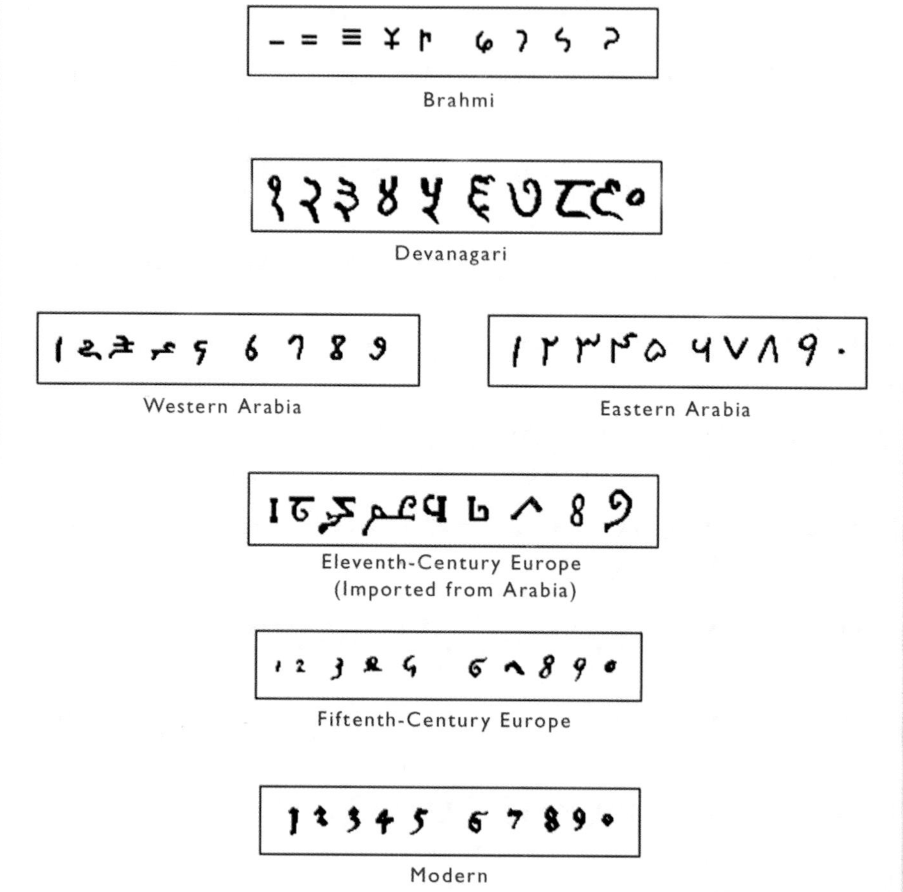

Brahmi

Devanagari

Western Arabia

Eastern Arabia

Eleventh-Century Europe
(Imported from Arabia)

Fifteenth-Century Europe

Modern

This chart shows the evolution of Hindi-Arabic numerals that are used in the West today. The numerals first appeared in India in the first century AD in the Brahmi script (except the zero, which came around 600). Over several centuries and through several variations, they evolved into a form known as the Devanagari script, which the Muslim Empire imported in the seventh century. There, two competing variants, Eastern Arab and Western Arab, emerged. The latter was exported to Europe by the eleventh century, where it passed through two major changes before taking its current form.

merely indicates the absence of a number that has an actual value. Most ancient cultures, including the Babylonians and Greeks, did not see the value of having a number that would signify nothing. Today, we are so familiar with using the number zero that we cannot comprehend what a strange concept it would have seemed to scholars first studying the Hindi system of numbers.

Al-Khwarizmi describes the Hindi numerals and the place value system in his treatise. A Latin translation of the work, as quoted by Ifrah, begins by stating al-Khwarizmi's purpose: "We have decided to explain Indian calculating techniques using the nine characters and to show how, because of their simplicity and conciseness, these characters are capable of expressing any number." Al-Khwarizmi does not neglect the zero, "the tenth figure in the shape of a circle" used "so as not to confuse the positions." He also outlines basic addition, subtraction, multiplication, division, and a few other mathematical functions using the Hindi system.

Muslim scholars and scribes were slow to adopt Hindi numerals. Many were unwilling to give up their traditional methods of writing and calculating amounts. It took even longer for the system to be introduced to Europe.

Al-Khwarizmi's treatise was translated into Latin during the twelfth century. The Latin version, however, is known to be significantly different from al-Khwarizmi's original. It was titled *Algoritmi de Numero Indorum* (Al-Khwarizmi

Concerning the Indian Art of Reckoning). In Latin, al-Khwarizmi's name was first transcribed as Alchoarismi, and it gradually evolved into Algorismi, Algorismus, Algorisme, Algoritmi, and finally Algorism and Algorithm. Scholars of late medieval Europe used the term "algorism" in reference to mathematical operations using the new Arabic system of numbers and system of calculation. Today, "algorithm" is a general term for the procedure of solving a mathematical problem, usually by using a precise series of steps. Algorithms in computer programs instruct the computer as to which steps to perform and in what sequence to complete a task.

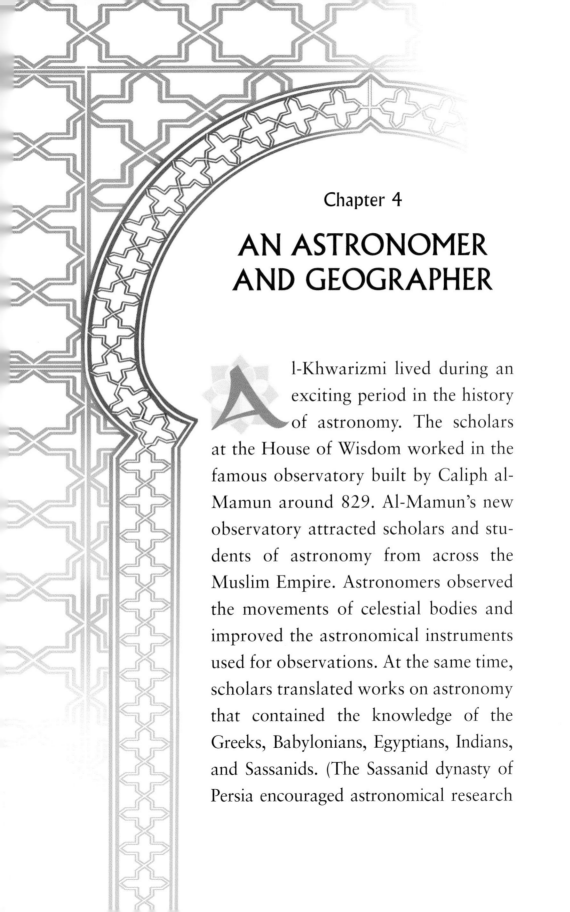

Chapter 4

AN ASTRONOMER AND GEOGRAPHER

l-Khwarizmi lived during an exciting period in the history of astronomy. The scholars at the House of Wisdom worked in the famous observatory built by Caliph al-Mamun around 829. Al-Mamun's new observatory attracted scholars and students of astronomy from across the Muslim Empire. Astronomers observed the movements of celestial bodies and improved the astronomical instruments used for observations. At the same time, scholars translated works on astronomy that contained the knowledge of the Greeks, Babylonians, Egyptians, Indians, and Sassanids. (The Sassanid dynasty of Persia encouraged astronomical research

between the third and seventh centuries.) Muslim astronomers built on this knowledge and applied it to both academic and practical purposes. Astronomical observations and calculations were used for calendars, timekeeping, horoscopes, and determination of precise latitudes and longitudes for locations.

ANCIENT ASTRONOMY

Humans have practiced astronomy since the very dawn of civilization. An understanding of the progression of the sun enabled people to predict the seasons and judge when to plant and harvest crops. The prehistoric monument Stonehenge, for example, functioned as an observatory as early as 3000 BC. The ancient Egyptians worshipped the stars, and they aligned the pyramids according to the positions of the stars.

The Babylonians were the first to develop an advanced form of astronomy. They recorded their observations and

Royal interest in astronomy, coupled with the demand for precise tables for preparing calendars for religious and secular purposes, spurred the establishment of observatories across the Muslim Empire from as early as the eighth century. Al-Khwarizmi worked in the observatory at the House of Wisdom during the time of al-Mamun. This illustration portrays thirteenth-century astronomer Nasireddin (standing) at work in his observatory at Maragha in Persia. It was one of the most impressive observatories at the time.

calculations on cuneiform tablets. As early as 1800 BC, Babylonian astronomers began to develop a solar calendar that marked the phases of the moon. They were able to predict eclipses and chart the courses of the planets Mercury, Venus, Mars, Jupiter, and Saturn.

Greek astronomers incorporated the discoveries of the Babylonians and greatly contributed to the theoretical knowledge of astronomy. One of the earliest Greek astronomers, Thales of Miletus (624–547 BC) may have studied at a Babylonian school around 640 BC. The Greeks often used the geometry of circles and spheres in their astronomy. Eudoxus of Cnidus (ca. 400–347 BC) was the first Greek astronomer to try to explain the movement of heavenly bodies. In about 370 BC, he introduced the theory that the sun, moon, stars, and planets were affixed to a number of huge transparent spheres, one nested inside the next. They revolved in various ways with the motionless Earth at their center. Aristotle and Apollonius of Perga used this model of the cosmos as the basis for their astronomical work. Greek astronomers of the third and second centuries BC worked on a catalog of star positions, methods for determining the magnitudes and relative distances of the sun and moon, and the means of measuring arc length.

The two greatest Greek astronomers were Hipparchus (190–120 BC) and Ptolemy. Hipparchus theorized that celestial bodies orbited around Earth following the paths

Eudoxus of Cnidus authored this second-century BC illustrated papyrus, detailing his observations on the movement of the heavenly bodies. He introduced mathematics into the study of astronomy and further revolutionized the field by building the first known observatory.

of various circles. He measured the solar year with only a six-minute discrepancy, and cataloged the positions of more than 1,000 stars. Ptolemy refined Hipparchus's work on the lunar cycle and devised an original theory of planetary motion. Ptolemy compiled Greek knowledge of astronomy as well as his own theories in a work called the *Almagest*. Ptolemy's *Almagest* was the defining work on astronomical theory until the sixteenth century.

This is a thirteenth-century copy of the Arabic translation of *Almagest*, Ptolemy's treatise on planetary motion. Written in Greek as *Hé Megele Syntaxis* (The Great Treatise) in the second century BC, the work was translated into Arabic as *Al-Kitabu-l-mijisti* (The Great Book) by Ishaq Hunayn in the ninth century. *Algamest* is a Latinized form of the Arabic title. Ptolemy *(inset)* wrote other influential treatises on geography, astrology, and music.

Muslim scholars first translated the *Almagest* into Arabic in 800. Al-Hajjaj, one of al-Khwarizmi's colleagues at the House of Wisdom, completed a superior translation in 827 to 828. Muslim astronomers accepted Ptolemy's model of the heavens revolving around a stationary Earth. They did not attempt to improve the theories behind Greek astronomy. Instead, they refined the calculations and observational data of star charts and planetary motion.

AL-KHWARIZMI'S ASTRONOMICAL WORKS

The study of astronomy in the Muslim Empire began in 771, when an Indian traveler brought a work called *Sindhind* to Baghdad. According to al-Biruni, the *Sindhind* was a Sanskrit version of the *Brahmasiddhanta*, which was written in 628 by the eminent Indian astronomer and mathematician Brahmagupta. Caliph al-Mansur ordered that the work be translated into Arabic. Ibrahim al-Fazazr, the first Muslim astronomer, completed the translation, titled *Zij al-Sindhind*, around 800. *Zij* means "set of astronomical tables."

Al-Khwarizmi's astronomical work, also titled *Zij al-Sindhind*, was a revision of the original version. He incorporated elements of Greek astronomy and also made his own original contributions. Over the course of his career, he worked on two editions of his *Zij*. There is no Arabic version of the work still in existence. Even in Latin translation, though, it is the earliest Arabic work on astronomy that survives in anything like its original form.

Historians have been able to deduce much of the contents of al-Khwarizmi's *Zij*. Around 1000, the Spanish Muslim astronomer Maslama al-Majriti, who lived in Córdoba, produced a revised version of the work. His student Ibn al-Saffar may have added further revisions. Adelard of Bath translated this version into Latin in the twelfth century.

Muslim astronomers who came after al-Khwarizmi wrote commentaries on his *Zij* and made references to it in their work. The astronomer al-Farghani produced a criticism of *Zij* in the second half of the ninth century. Al-Muthanna mentions al-Farghani's book in his own commentary on *Zij*, written in the tenth century. Neither work survives in Arabic, although al-Muthanna's commentary exists in Hebrew and Latin translations. In the introduction, al-Muthanna states that "the explanations in al-Farghani's treatise [lacked] completeness." It is possible that al-Muthanna's commentary is merely an expansion of al-Farghani's criticism. In any case, al-Muthanna presented his points in the form of questions and answers concerning al-Khwarizmi's *Zij* and gives a fair idea of the scope of the original work.

Al-Khwarizmi's *Zij* consisted of tables and instructions for calculating the positions of the sun, moon, and planets. Other tables addressed calculations for eclipses, visibility of the moon, and trigonometric functions. Al-Khwarizmi also discussed various calendars and methods for determining the time of day.

In his book *The History of Algebra*, B. L. van der Waerden quotes the historian Ibn al-Qifti on the sources al-Khwarizmi drew on for his *Zij*:

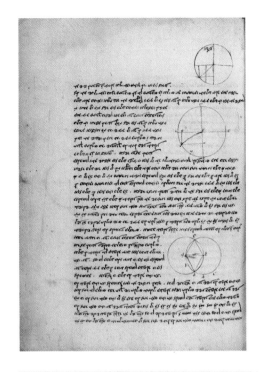

> He used in his tables the mean motions of the *Sindhind*, but he deviated from it in the equations (of the planets) and in the obliquity (of the ecliptic). He fixed the equations according to the method of the Persians, and the declination of the sun according to the method of Ptolemy.

This is a page from al-Muthanna's *Commentary on the Astronomical Tables of Al-Khwarizmi*. Al-Muthanna was a leading Muslim scholar of the tenth century.

Ibn al-Qifti is saying, essentially, that al-Khwarizmi used Ptolemy's astronomy and the "method of the Persians" as well as the *Sindhind* in compiling the various tables. Al-Khwarizmi learned this "method of the Persians" from a Sassanid work, *Zij al-Shah* (The King's Astronomical Tables), written around 550.

This is a copper astrolabe from ninth-century Iraq. It is likely to have been of the same or similar design as those al-Khwarizmi used in his astronomical research. The astrolabe was the most important computational instrument of the Middle Ages. As such, craftsmen took great pride in making them, often signing the finest ones. This astrolabe was made by Ahmad Ibn Khalaf, whose name is inscribed on the instrument.

If a modern student of science were to travel back to al-Mamun's observatory, it is likely that he or she would not immediately recognize the instruments or the purpose of the structure. Telescopes had not yet been invented. Astronomers used instruments such as astrolabes, quadrants, sundials, and celestial globes to observe the motion of heavenly bodies.

Muslim astronomers made important advances in the development of these instruments. The astrolabe, the most important observational instrument of the time, was invented by the Greeks. Al-Fazari was the first Muslim astronomer to construct an astrolabe, probably in 777. Muslim scientists perfected the design of the astrolabe, and it was the primary instrument used for navigation until it was replaced by the quadrant in the eighteenth century.

The word "astrolabe" is derived from the Latin roots *astro*, for "star," and *labio*, for "finder." It consists of two plates. A solid plate called the tympan is engraved with lines representing the horizon, various altitudes, and other data for a certain latitude. It is overlaid with a rotating plate called the rete that has sections cut out to leave pointers representing the brightest stars in the sky. On the back is a movable sighting bar and an engraving of the circle of degrees. The astronomer measures the altitude of a certain star with the sighting bar, and then turns the rete on the other side of the astrolabe until the pointer for the star matches the corresponding altitude line on the tympan. By measuring the position of heavenly bodies, the astrolabe provided information for timekeeping, determination of geographical position, and astrological procedures.

Al-Khwarizmi wrote two works on the astrolabe, *Kitab 'Amal al-Asturlab* (Book on the Construction of the Astrolabe), and *Kitab al-'Amal bi'l-Asturlab* (Book on the Operation of the Astrolabe). Both have been lost. It is believed, however, that al-Farghani included al-Khwarizmi's *Book on the Operation of the Astrolabe* in one of his works. This section of al-Farghani's work explains how the astrolabe can be used to find the altitude of the sun, determine one's location, and solve various other astronomical problems.

Al-Khwarizmi also wrote a book called *Kitab al-Rukhama* (On the Sundial), which has also been lost. The precision of timekeeping devices such as the sundial was very important in the Muslim Empire for religious and administrative reasons. Observant Muslims offer prayers toward Mecca at five precise times every day. Muslim

This unsigned and undated celestial globe is thought to have been made by Ibrahim ibn Said al-Sahli around 1080. It has 1,004 stars arranged into forty-eight constellations in accordance with Ptolemy's *Almagest*. Celestial globes were used primarily as instructional aids. However, they were equally prized for their beauty.

The Science of Astrology

Astrology is the practice of predicting and analyzing events on Earth through interpretation of the positions of the stars and other celestial bodies. Through the history of civilization, many cultures have independently established systems of astrology, some of which are still used today. The Indians, Chinese, Egyptians, Babylonians, Greeks, and Mayans all developed unique astrological practices. Muslim astrology, like Arab mathematics and science, drew on many sources.

During the time of al-Khwarizmi, astrology was considered a precise science closely related to astronomy. Muslim astrologers frequently used the same instruments and mathematics as astronomers in charting the positions of heavenly bodies and calculating how their configuration at particular times might affect life on Earth. Many caliphs and government officials employed astrologers. They built observatories for charting the stars that were used by both astronomers and astrologers.

Astrology was popular with people of all classes throughout the Muslim Empire, but there were some who opposed the practice. Religious authorities argued that Islam centers around submission to the will of God and, therefore, prohibits making predictions. Some astronomers, such as al-Biruni, expressed doubt that studying the stars could truly foretell events on Earth. Despite these objections, astrologers could always find work predicting the outcome of events or determining the best times to begin certain activities, whether waging battles or digging wells. Even skeptics such as al-Biruni contributed to the huge body of astrological texts produced between the ninth and fourteenth centuries.

scientists used instruments and mathematical calculations in perfecting *'ilm al-miqat*, the "science of the fixed moments" or timekeeping. The indicator bar of the sundial is set so that it is parallel to the axis of the earth. It casts a shadow that changes in length and angle throughout the day. The shadow also changes throughout the cycle of a year. Muslim astronomers calculated shadow length and the corresponding height of the sun and recorded them in tables, which were distributed across the empire.

The Islamic faith also necessitated a precise calendar, which was devised by astronomers. A new lunar calendar was established in the seventh century. It measures the years following the Hijra, or Muhammad's move from Mecca to Medina. In the lunar calendar, the first appearance of the crescent moon marks the beginning of each month.

The study of calendars remained a subject of interest for Muslim astronomers. They were constantly looking for ways to revise the calendar to improve the accuracy of astronomical measurements. Al-Khwarizmi, for example, studied the Jewish calendar. He described it in a short treatise called *Istikhraj Ta'rikh al-Yahud* (About the Jewish Calendar), one of al-Khwarizmi's few Arabic texts that still exists. It is a well-researched work that gives historians insight into the development of the Jewish calendar. The Jewish calendar is based on both the solar and lunar cycles. In order to coordinate the two systems, a month is added to the year seven times during a nineteen-year cycle. The year begins with the month of Tishri, but a number of factors may delay the beginning of the month by a day. Al-Khwarizmi calculated the amount of time between the Jewish era—the time of the book of Genesis in the Bible—and the era of the Seleucid dynasty of the second and first centuries BC. He also states the rules for calculating longitudes of the sun and moon according to the Jewish calendar.

Al-Khwarizmi's *Kitab al-Ta'rikh* (Chronicle), was an astrological account of history rather than a purely astronomical work. It has been lost, but Muslim scholars cite it as a reference for certain historical events. Chronicle attempted to prove that history fulfills the predictions made by astrology. It included the horoscopes of various public figures. According to the tenth-century literary historian al-Isfahani, al-Khwarizmi once calculated the precise hour of the prophet Muhammad's birth by analyzing the events of his lifetime through astrology. *Chronicle* may have been the source for al-Isfahani's account.

GEOGRAPHY

Islamic religious practices also spurred the advancement of geography and mapmaking. In order to meet the requirement to face Mecca as they prayed, observant Muslims need to know their own precise geographic location in relation to Mecca.

During the reign of Caliph al-Mamun, al-Khwarizmi and sixty-nine other scholars executed "the form of the earth," the first Muslim map of the world and the heavens. He also wrote a book on geography called *Kitab Surat al-Ard*, one of his few works that survives in Arabic. Although the title literally means "Book of the Form of the Earth," most historians refer to it simply as al-Khwarizmi's *Geography*.

Geography mainly consists of lists of the latitudes and longitudes for more than 2,400 locations. It is divided into six sections: cities, mountains, seas, islands, the central points of certain geographical regions, and rivers. Entries for each section are arranged into seven "climata" based on latitude, and locations within each "clima" are listed according to longitude. Al-Khwarizmi gives details of the size and shape of mountains, seas, and islands, and he lists towns and any points of interest on the rivers.

Ptolemy also wrote a work called *Geography*, his most famous work after the *Almagest*. It discusses the techniques of mapmaking and lists latitudes and longitudes of locations for a map of the world. Ptolemy's *Geography* contains many inaccuracies, but his principles of mapmaking were scientifically sound. The work remained influential until the Renaissance.

Al-Khwarizmi included this map of the Nile River in his *Geography*. The lines across the map represent climate divisions, the highest one marking the equator.

Al-Khwarizmi consulted Ptolemy's *Geography* in writing his own. Al-Khwarizmi's work includes many of the same locations, some with identical latitudes and longitudes. But al-Khwarizmi's *Geography* is not a mere revision of Ptolemy's. The entries are organized according to a different system, and al-Khwarizmi's map differs significantly from Ptolemy's work. It is generally more accurate than Ptolemy's map, especially in the regions of the Muslim Empire, Africa, and Asia.

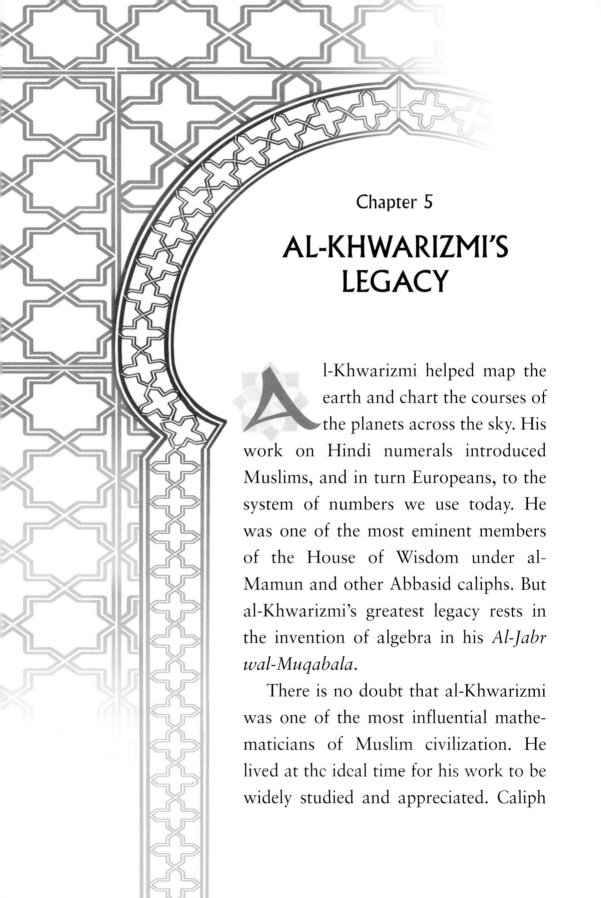

Chapter 5

AL-KHWARIZMI'S LEGACY

l-Khwarizmi helped map the earth and chart the courses of the planets across the sky. His work on Hindi numerals introduced Muslims, and in turn Europeans, to the system of numbers we use today. He was one of the most eminent members of the House of Wisdom under al-Mamun and other Abbasid caliphs. But al-Khwarizmi's greatest legacy rests in the invention of algebra in his *Al-Jabr wal-Muqabala*.

There is no doubt that al-Khwarizmi was one of the most influential mathematicians of Muslim civilization. He lived at thc idcal time for his work to be widely studied and appreciated. Caliph al-Mamun supported research and the translation of ancient texts, which helped lay a foundation for further achievements by Muslim scientists. Scholars who came after al-Khwarizmi recognized the caliber of *Al-Jabr wal-Muqabala*. They made copies that they passed on to other mathematicians and preserved in libraries and universities. Mathematicians such as al-Karaji (953–1029), and Umar al-Khayyam made further advancements in the study of algebra.

Historians acknowledge al-Khwarizmi's influence in mathematics, but they do not all agree that he was necessarily a great mathematician. There has been considerable speculation about the sources that al-Khwarizmi studied while writing his *Al-Jabr wal-Muqabala*. Did al-Khwarizmi truly invent algebra, or did he merely compile and systemize the elements of algebra from the mathematic work of other cultures?

Mathematicians after al-Khwarizmi acknowledged him as the founder of the discipline of algebra. The tenth-century mathematician al-Kamil, for example, referred to al-Khwarizmi as "the one who was the first to succeed in a book of algebra and al-muqabala and who pioneered and invented all the principles in it," as quoted by Roshdi Rashed in *The Development of Arabic Mathematics*. Nevertheless, many historians have attempted to trace possible precursors to the mathematics in *Al-Jabr wal-Muqabala*. Although many theories have been put forth, no historian has been able to conclusively prove al-Khwarizmi's debt to any single source.

Several ancient cultures developed quadratic equations or other elements of algebra. Historians most often suggest that al-Khwarizmi may have used Greek, Indian, Babylonian, or Hebrew sources.

In particular, scholars debate whether al-Khwarizmi was familiar with Euclid's *Elements* and whether it influenced his *Al-Jabr wal-Muqabala*. Al-Hajjaj, the translator of Ptolemy's *Almagest*, also completed two different translations of *The Elements*, one under Harun al-Rashid and the other under al-Mamun. Al-Khwarizmi used geometric proofs for his equations, which indicates that he had studied some geometrical works. Al-Khwarizmi's style is very different from that of Euclid, though—he does not use formal axioms and definitions. The scholar Solomon Gandz, as quoted in B. L. van der Waerden's *History of Algebra*, hypothesizes that al-Khwarizmi purposely distances himself from Euclid's *Elements*.

Euclid and his geometry, though available in a good translation by his colleague, is entirely ignored by him when he

Recognized in the West for his invention of algebra, al-Khwarizmi is celebrated as a heroic figure in Muslim countries, especially in Iran. Each year, Iran holds a Khwarizmi festival in which it gives awards to Iranian and international scholars for outstanding scientific and industrial research. This statue of al-Khwarizmi is at the Mirkabir University of Technology in Tehran, Iran.

writes on geometry. On the contrary, in the preface to his *Algebra* al-Khowarizmi distinctly emphasizes his purpose of writing a popular treatise that in contradiction to Greek theoretical mathematics, will serve the practical ends and needs of the people in their affairs of inheritance and legacies, in their law suits, in trade and commerce, in the surveying of lands and in the digging of canals. Hence, al-Khowarizmi appears to us not as a pupil of the Greeks but, quite to the contrary, as the antagonist of al-Hajjaj and the Greek school, as the representative of the native popular sciences.

Gandz puts forth an interesting theory, but this is only his own interpretation of al-Khwarizmi's motives. There is absolutely no evidence that al-Khwarizmi intentionally neglected the Greek classics.

Al-Khwarizmi wrote about Hindi numerals and used the Indian *Sindhind* as the basis for *Zij*. Some Indian influence can be identified in his *Al-Jabr wal-Muqabala*. In the second section, he uses a value of π and gives a method for finding the circumference of a circle, which may have been taken from Indian sources. Indian mathematicians were familiar with quadratic equations like al-Khwarizmi's. But al-Khwarizmi's presentation of algebraic principles cannot be traced directly to any specific Indian work.

Solomon Gandz put forth the theory that *Al-Jabr wal-Muqabala* borrowed material from an early Hebrew geometry treatise, *Mishnat ha-Middot*. Al-Khwarizmi's work on the

Adelard of Bath

Adelard (or Aethelard) of Bath was a twelfth-century scholar and philosopher who has been called the first English scientist. He studied and taught in France before leaving to spend many years traveling. He visited the famous medical school in Salerno, Italy, and proceeded on to Sicily. Arabs from North Africa had conquered the island in 965 and controlled it for about a century, and some Islamic influence remained. Adelard may have become fluent in Arabic in Sicily, or he may have learned the language while visiting Spain in his subsequent travels.

Adelard is known in particular for his study of Islamic philosophy and science. He translated a version of al-Khwarizmi's *Zij* into Latin, after which it was known as the *Kharismian Tables*. He also made two translations of Euclid's *Elements* from Arabic into Latin. One of the original Arabic versions is believed to have been al-Hajjaj's translation from Greek. He also translated works on astronomy and astrology. Paralleling al-Khwarizmi, Adelard wrote treatises on the astrolabe, cast horoscopes for members of the royal family, and advocated the use of Hindi-Arabic numerals and the zero. Adelard is believed to be the author of a mathematical treatise that, in part, discusses Indian methods of arithmetic. It has been speculated that it was based on al-Khwarizmi's work. Adelard was also a philosopher who promulgated the doctrine of indifference.

Like the scholars of the House of Wisdom of an earlier age, Adelard translated classic works and wrote his own. The circulation of these works contributed to a new age of learning.

This table for determining the times of the daylight prayers for latitude 33° north (Baghdad) was included in one of al-Khwarizmi's treatises on the construction and use of the astrolabe. Together with other Muslim astronomers who calculated the latitude and longitude of important Muslim cities, al-Khwarizmi made it easier for observant Muslims to know which way to turn to face Mecca during prayer, as required by the Qur'an.

Jewish calendar shows that he was familiar with Jewish scholarship. Gandz, who studied the *Mishnat ha-Middot*, estimates that it was composed in the second century. Other scholars, however, believe that the work was actually written after al-Khwarizmi's time.

Gandz's discussion of al-Khwarizmi and his supposed rejection of Euclid's *Elements* does bring up al-Khwarizmi's stated goal of producing a work that would serve the needs of ordinary people. Almost all of al-Khwarizmi's works were intended to serve a practical purpose. His *Geography* describes a map of the world. *Zij* provides tables and instructions for making astronomical calculations. The treatise on Hindi numerals systematically outlines the decimal number system and introduces the zero. Al-Khwarizmi's works on the astrolabe and sundial, perhaps written during the construction of al-Mamun's observatory, discuss practical aspects of observing the heavens. Even his *Chronicle* attempts to show that astrology is a rational branch of science. Unlike his colleague al-Kindi, al-Khwarizmi apparently never ventured into imprecise fields such as philosophy or religious thought.

Al-Khwarizmi's works were widely circulated after his death. His *Geography* remained influential in Muslim lands through the fourteenth century, although it was Ptolemy's *Geography* that most influenced Western mapmakers. *Al-Jabr wal-Muqabala* and a version of his treatise on Hindi numerals were eventually translated into Latin and greatly influenced Western mathematics. *Zij* was the first work of its type to be translated into Latin. Sections of the *Zij* were later included in the *Toledan Tables*, an assortment of astronomical tables drawn from the works of Muslim astronomers. This work was influential in Europe for more than 100 years.

Although al-Khwarizmi's name is not familiar to the general public, his work is highly respected by historians and mathematicians. G. J. Toomer writes in *The Dictionary of Scientific Biography*, "Al-Khwarizmi's scientific achievements were at best mediocre," but most experts hold al-Khwarizmi in much higher regard. In his monumental work *History of the Arabs*, Philip Hitti writes of al-Khwarizmi, "One of the greatest scientific minds of Islam, he influenced mathematical thought to a greater extent than any other medieval writer." The renowned historian of science Roshdi Rashed rejects the idea that al-Khwarizmi's work was derived from older sources. He writes in *The Development of Arabic Mathematics* that "it is impossible to overstress the originality of al-Khwarizmi's algebra, which did not rise from any 'arithmetical' tradition."

Mohammad Khan highly praises al-Khwarizmi and his legacy to the Western world in his book *A Brief Survey of*

This is the title page of a fourteenth-century Latin translation of al-Khwarizmi's *Kitab al-Jabr wal-Muqabala*, showing a Latinized spelling of the great Muslim scholar's name. It is likely that Adelard of Bath was the translator. It wasn't until al-Khwarizmi's work was translated into Latin that it began to seriously spread throughout Europe, greatly advancing the study of mathematics.

Muslim Contribution to Science and Culture (as quoted by al-Daffa in *The Muslim Contribution to Mathematics*).

> In the foremost rank of mathematicians of all times stands al-Khwarizmi. He composed the oldest works on arithmetic and algebra. They were the principal source of mathematical knowledge for centuries to come both in the East and the West.

In *The Universal History of Numbers*, Georges Ifrah sums up al-Khwarizmi's contributions to the modern world.

> Unbeknown to him, al-Khwarizmi provided the name for a fundamental branch of modern mathematics, and gave his own name to the science of algorithms, the basis for one of the practical and theoretical activities of computing. What more can be said about this great scholar's influence?

TIMELINE

622

The prophet Muhammad migrates from Mecca to Medina, an event known as the Hijra.

632

The prophet Muhammad dies. The caliphate is founded.

762

Baghdad is founded.

780

Al-Khwarizmi is born.

786

Harun al-Rashid becomes the fifth caliph of the Abbasid dynasty.

813

Al-Mamun becomes caliph.

813–833

Al-Khwarizmi completes his *Kitab al-Jabr wal-Muqabala* and *Zij*.

833

Al-Mutasim becomes caliph.

(continued on following page)

(continued from previous page)

836

Rebellion forces the caliph to move the capital to Samarra.

842

Al-Wathiq becomes caliph.

847

Al-Khwarizmi is present at al-Wathiq's death. Al-Mutawakkil becomes caliph.

848

Al-Mutawakkil discontinues the *mihna* begun by al-Mamun.

circa 850

Al-Khwarizmi dies.

861

Al-Mutawakkil is assassinated.

892

Baghdad is reestablished as the capital.

circa 1000

Al-Majriti brings al-Khwarizmi's works to Muslim Spain.

1258

Mongols sack Baghdad and put an end to the Abbasid dynasty.

GLOSSARY

acrophonic Using a symbol to phonetically represent the initial sound of the name of an object.

algebra The branch of mathematics in which numbers and other elements of equations can be represented by letters.

astrolabe An instrument used to observe and calculate the positions of the sun and other celestial bodies.

astrology The practice of predicting and analyzing events on Earth through interpretation of the position of the stars and other celestial bodies.

axiom A statement that is accepted as truth without formal proof.

caliph The leader of a Muslim state, regarded as the successor of Muhammad.

cuneiform A script once used in Babylonia and other ancient societies.

eclipse The obscuring of the light of one celestial body by another.

geometry The branch of mathematics that examines points, lines, angles, surfaces, and solids.

hypotenuse The side of a right triangle that is opposite the right angle.

legacy Something passed on from an ancestor or predecessor.

quadratic equation A mathematical equation in which one or more of the unknown quantities is squared; none of the terms are raised to a higher power.

terrestrial Relating to the land.

theorem A mathematical statement that has been formally proven to be true.

treatise a written discourse on a particular subject, often thorough and systematic.

trigonometry The branch of mathematics that deals with the calculations based on the relationships between the angles and sides of triangles.

FOR MORE INFORMATION

The British Society for the History of Mathematics
20 Dunvegan Close,
Exeter, Devon EX4 4AF
England
(+44) 01256 813002
Web site: http://www.bshm.org

Canadian Society for the History and Philosophy
  of Mathematics
Department of Mathematics and Computer Science
Adelphi University
Garden City, NY 11530
(516) 877-4496
Web site: http://www.cshpm.org

Museum of the History of Science
Broad Street
Oxford OX1 3AZ
England
(+44) 01865 277280
Web site: http://www.mhs.ox.ac.uk

Omar Center for Cultural and Educational Outreach—
  Omar ibn Khattab Foundation
1025 W. Exposition Blvd.
Los Angeles, CA 90007
(310) 364 2091
Web site: http://www.omarfoundation.org

WEB SITES

Due to the changing nature of Internet links, the Rosen Publishing Group, Inc., has developed an online list of Web sites related to the subject of this book. This site is updated regularly. Please use this link to access the list:

http://www.rosenlinks.com/gmps/khwa

FOR FURTHER READING

Heide, Florence Parry. *House of Wisdom*. New York, NY:
DK Publishing, 1999.

Kheirabadi, Masoud. *Islam*. New York, NY: Chelsea House
Publications, 2004.

Mantin, Peter. *The Islamic World: Beliefs and Civilizations,
600–1600*. New York, NY: Cambridge University
Press, 1993.

McCaughrean, Geraldine. *One Thousand and One Arabian
Nights*. New York, NY: Oxford University Press, 2000.

Nasr, Seyyed Hossein. *Islamic Science: An Illustrated Study*.
Chicago, IL: Kazi Publications, 1976.

BIBLIOGRAPHY

Daffa, Ali Abdullah al-. *The Muslim Contribution to Mathematics*. Atlantic Highlands, NJ: Humanities Press, 1977.

Goldstein, Bernard R., ed. *Ibn al-Muthanna's Commentary on the Astronomical Tales of al-Khwarizmi*. New Haven, CT: Yale University Press, 1967.

Hill, Fred James, and Nicolas Awde. *A History of the Islamic World*. New York, NY: Hippocrene Books, 2003.

Hitti, Philip. *History of the Arabs*. New York, NY: Palgrave Macmillan, 2002.

Hourani, Albert. *A History of the Arab Peoples*. Cambridge, MA: Belknap Press of Harvard University Press, 1991.

Ifrah, Georges. *The Universal History of Numbers: From Prehistory to the Invention of the Computer*. New York, NY: John Wiley & Sons, 2000.

Lapidus, Ira M. *A History of Islamic Societies*. New York, NY: Cambridge University Press, 1988.

O'Connor, J. J., and E. F. Robertson. "Adelard of Bath." University of Saint Andrews School of Mathematics and Statistics. November 1999. Retrieved February 20, 2005 (http://www-groups.dcs.st-and.ac.uk/~history/Mathematicians/Adelard.html).

Rashed, Roshdi. *The Development of Arabic Mathematics: Between Arithmetic and Algebra.* Boston, MA: Kluwer Academic Publishers, 1994.

Saunders, J. J. *A History of Medieval Islam.* Boston, MA: Routledge and Kegan Paul, 1972.

Semaan, Khalil I., ed. *Islam and the Medieval West: Aspects of Intercultural Relations.* Albany, NY: State University of New York Press, 1980.

Spuler, Bertold. *The Age of the Caliphs: History of the Muslim World.* Princeton, NJ: Markus Wiener Publishers, 1995.

Toomer, Gerald J. "Al-Khwarizmi, Abu Ja'far Muhammad ibn Musa." Edited by Charles C. Gillispie. Vol. 7 of *Dictionary of Scientific Biography.* New York, NY: Charles Scribner's Sons, 1981.

Turner, Howard R. *Science in Medieval Islam.* Austin, TX: University of Texas Press, 1997.

Van der Waerden, B. L. *The History of Algebra: From al-Khwarizmi to Emmy Noether.* New York, NY: Springer-Verlag, 1985.

INDEX

About the Author

Corona Brezina is a writer and researcher who lives in Chicago, Illinois. A graduate of Oberlin College and Conservatory, she has written more than a dozen books, many of which focus on the histories and cultures of various countries around the world. She has a keen interest in the development of Western civilization and how various cultures contributed to it. She remains fascinated by Al-Khwarizmi's significant role in advancing the study of mathematics and human understanding of the world.

About the Consultant

Munir A. Shaikh, executive director of the Council on Islamic Education (CIE), reviewed this book. The CIE is a nonadvocacy, academic research institute that provides consulting services and academic resources related to teaching about world history and world religions. http://www.cie.org.

Photo Credits

Cover, p.33 1983 stamp, Soviet Union; p. 7 Snark/Art Resource, NY; pp. 8–9 Map by András Bereznay, http://www.historyonmaps.com; p. 13 Egyptian National Library, Cairo, Egypt, Giraudon/Bridgeman Art Library; pp. 15, 73 Réunion des Musées Nationaux/Art Resource, NY; p. 17 © The British Library: Or. 11676 f.113; p. 19 © 2004 Werner Forman/TopFoto/The Image Works; p. 20 © The British Museum/HIP/The Image Works; pp. 24, 94 Bildarchiv Preussischer Kulturbesitz/Art Resource, NY; pp. 26, 52, 74 (inset) Erich Lessing/Art Resource, NY; pp. 28, 41, 82, 93, background tiles courtesy of Mosaic House, New York; p. 31 © Jane Sweeney/Lonely Planet Images; p. 34 © Ann Ronan Picture Library/HIP/The Image Works; p. 36 1994 stamp, Syria/Stamp Courtesy Magan Stamps; p. 38 © Ann Ronan Picture Library/HIP/Art Resource, NY; p. 42 SEF/Art Resource, NY; p. 45 Photo and collections of the Bibliothèque Nationale et Universitaire, Strasbourg, MS.4.247, fol. 11b; p. 47 © British Library/HIP/Art Resource, NY; p. 50 Art Resource, NY; p. 53 Scala/Art Resource, NY; p. 56 The Bodleian Library, University of Oxford, MS. Huntington 214, title page; p. 59 The Bodleian Library, University of Oxford, MS. Huntington 214, fol. 17r (detail); p. 63 Museum of Islamic Art, Cairo, Egypt/Bridgeman Art Library; p. 66 Modified from Karl Menninger, "Number Words and Number Symbols; A Cultural History of Numbers." Cambridge, MA: The M.I.T. Press, 1969; p. 70 British Library, London, UK/Bridgeman Art Library; pp. 74, 81 Bibliothèque Nationale de France; p. 77 The Bodleian Library, University of Oxford, Michael 400, fol. 53v; p. 78 Bibliothèque Nationale de Cartes et Plans, Paris, France/Bridgeman Art Library; p. 86 Photo and collections of the Bibliothèque Nationale et Universitaire, Strasbourg, MS.4.247, fols. 30b-31a; p. 91 Photo courtesy of Matthias Tomczak; p. 97 The Bodleian Library, University of Oxford, MS. Lyell 52, fol. 21r.

Designer: Les Kanturek; Photo Researcher: Gabriel Caplan